910

Among pianists of the front rank, Alfred Brendel is rare in being able to express himself with clarity and style in words as well as music, bringing to his writing the same intellectual power and fine sensibility that distinguish his playing.

In this important book Brendel examines subjects central to his repertoire. Besides further exploration of the music of Beethoven, Liszt and Busoni, there are chapters on Mozart, Schumann and Bach. Two major lectures included here have become known through BBC broadcasts: a detailed study of Schubert's last three piano sonatas, and a diverting investigation of musical humour. Brendel also offers some original views on programme-planning, makes a strong case for live recordings and discusses the performing style of Wilhelm Furtwängler and Artur Schnabel.

Always illuminating and challenging *Music Sounded Out* should appeal to both the specialist and the music lover. It provides not only stimulating reading but an insight into the exceptional mind of a great pianist.

D1343356

*Also by Alfred Brendel and published by Robson Books*

**Musical Thoughts and Afterthoughts**

# Alfred Brendel

# *Music*

# *Sounded*

# *Out*

## Essays, Lectures,
## Interviews, Afterthoughts

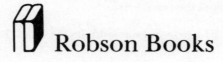

**Robson Books**

This Robson paperback edition first published in 1995

First published in Great Britain in 1990 by Robson Books Ltd, Bolsover House, 5-6 Clipstone Street, London W1P 8LE

Copyright © 1990 Alfred Brendel
The right of Alfred Brendel to be identified as author of this work has been asserted by him in accordance with the Copyright, Designs and Patents Act 1988

**British Library Cataloguing in Publication Data**
A catalogue record for this title is available from the British Library

ISBN 0 86051 666 0 (hbk)
    0 86051 986 4 (pbk)

All rights reserved. No part of this publication may be reproduced, stored in a retrieval system, or transmitted in any form or by any means, electronic, mechanical, photocopying, recording or otherwise, without the prior permission in writing of the publishers.

Printed in Great Britain by St Edmundsbury Press Ltd, Bury St Edmunds, Suffolk.

# Contents

# Preface

This book continues where *Musical Thoughts and Afterthoughts* (1976) ended. It gathers again comments on music, musicians and matters of performance written by a musical practitioner who has little inclination to be autobiographical. Even in his most personal and specific statements, he hopes to draw attention to problems less personal and specific than his own, and to relate his observations or musings to a larger context.

The pieces assembled here are informed by self-doubt, and frequently motivated by self-help. Where advice is offered, it has been aimed at myself in the first place; I shall be glad if it proves of value to others. Essays are not oracles. I like to see them, at least potentially, as works in progress; in this, they resemble musical performances which continue to call for new insight, and improvement. My readers and listeners may rest assured that I do not subscribe to the notion of absolute truth, even if I am keen to pursue relative truths with as much passion as my habitual scepticism will permit.

Of these essays, several started life as sleeve notes for my own records; a few more were written as programme notes for my recitals. Most have been extensively expanded and revised. 'Must Classical Music be Entirely Serious? (The Sublime in Reverse)' was first given as the Darwin Lecture at Cambridge in 1984, while 'Schubert's Last Sonatas' was delivered, in an abridged version, as the 1989 Edward Boyle Lecture at the Royal Society of Arts in London. In similar or considerably different form, one or more of these pieces appeared in the *New York Review*, *Die Zeit*, *The Times Literary Supplement*, the *Piano Quarterly*, the *Gramophone*, *HiFidelity* magazine, the *Musical Times* and *Musica*. Eugene Hartzell's translation for Philips of my original German text served as a point of departure for the following: 'A Mozart Player Gives Himself Advice', 'Beethoven's New Style', 'The Text and its

1

Guardians', 'Liszt's Bitterness of Heart' and 'A Case for Live Recordings'. All the others were written in English, or translated from the German by myself. The dates of the original versions are given at the end of each chapter. My thanks go to all the publishers concerned.

Among the many people to whom I owe gratitude, I should like to mention Frank Kermode who instigated my Darwin Lecture, Sir Isaiah Berlin who looked over my shoulder when I started to write it down, Sir Ernst Gombrich and Klaus Heinrich who provided me with illuminating material on laughter, and Hans Keller who, already terminally ill, had the patience to listen to a run-through. Next to Hans, another conversation partner now deceased was Konrad Wolff, whose interview on my queries concerning Schnabel is reprinted here. The Floersheim Collection in Basle kindly allowed me to examine the autograph of Schubert's last three sonatas. Bernard Jacobson, whose views on repeats differ from mine, helped me to clarify my own standpoint. Finally, I feel indebted to Monika Möllering, William Kinderman, James Webster, Antony Beaumont and Leonard Stein for their constructive suggestions, and to my editor Carolyn Fearnside for her empathy and attention.

A.B.
*London, 1990*

# A Mozart Player Gives Himself Advice

*Unmistakably, Mozart takes singing as his starting-point, and from this issues the uninterrupted melodiousness which shimmers through his compositions like the lovely forms of a woman through the folds of a thin dress.*

FERRUCCIO BUSONI

Let this be the first warning to the Mozart performer: piano playing, be it ever so faultless, must not be considered sufficient. Mozart's piano works should be for the player a receptacle full of latent musical possibilities which often go far beyond the purely pianistic. It is not the limitations of Mozart's pianoforte (which I refuse to accept) that point the way, but rather Mozart's dynamism, colourfulness and expressiveness in operatic singing, in the orchestra, in ensembles of all kinds. For example, the first movement of Mozart's Sonata in A minor K.310 is to me a piece for symphony orchestra; the second movement resembles a vocal scene with a dramatic middle section, and the finale could be transcribed into a wind divertimento with no trouble at all.

In Mozart's piano concertos, the sound of the piano is set off more sharply against that of the orchestra. Here the human voice and the orchestral solo instrument will be the main setters of standards for the pianist. From the Mozart singer he will learn not only to sing but also to 'speak' clearly and with meaning, to characterize, to act and react; from the string player to think in terms of up-bow and down-bow; and from the flautist or oboist to shape fast passages in a variety of articulations, instead of delivering them up to an automatic non-legato or, worse still, to an undeviating legato such as the old complete edition prescribed time and again without a shred of authenticity.

A singing line and sensuous beauty, important as they may be in Mozart, are not, however, the sole sources of bliss. To tie Mozart to a few traits is to diminish him. That great composers have manifold things to say and can use contradictions to their advantage should be evident in performances of his music. There has been altogether too much readiness to reduce Mozart to Schumann's 'floating Greek gracefulness' or Wagner's 'genius of light and love'. Finding a balance between freshness and urbanity ('He did not remain simple and did not grow over-refined,' said Busoni), force and transparency, unaffectedness and irony, aloofness and intimacy, between freedom and set patterns, passion and grace, abandonment and style – among the labours of the Mozart player, this is only rewarded by a stroke of good luck.

\*

What is it that marks out Mozart's music? An attempt to draw a dividing-line between Haydn and Mozart could perhaps help to answer the question. Mozart sometimes comes astonishingly close to Haydn, and Haydn to Mozart, and they shared their musical accomplishments in brotherly fashion; but they were fundamentally different in nature. I see in Haydn and Mozart the antithesis between instrumental and vocal, motif and melody, C.P.E. and J.C. Bach, adagio and andante, caesuras (amusing and startling) and connections (seamless), daring and balance, the surprise of the unexpected and the surprise of the expected. From tranquillity, Haydn plunges deep into agitation, while Mozart does the reverse, aiming at tranquillity from nervousness.

Mozart's nervous energy – his fingers were constantly drumming on the nearest chair-back – can be recognized in the fidgety or spirited agitation of many final movements, as one heard them in performances by Edwin Fischer, Bruno Walter or Artur Schnabel. When Busoni denies Mozart any nervousness, I have to disagree. Like melodiousness shimmering through the folds of a dress, 'chaos' now and then, even in Mozart, can be 'shimmering through the veil of order' (Novalis).

The perfection of that order, the security of Mozart's sense of form, is, as Busoni puts it, 'almost inhuman'. Let us therefore never lose sight of the humanity of this music, even when it gives itself an official and general air. The unimpeachability of his form is always balanced by the palpability of his sound, the miracle of his sound mixtures, the resoluteness of his energy, the living spirit, the heartbeat, the unsentimental warmth of his feeling.

*

Between Haydn the explorer and adventurer, and Schubert the sleepwalker, I see both Mozart and Beethoven as architects. But how differently they built! From the beginning of a piece, Beethoven places stone upon stone, constructing and justifying his edifice as it were in accordance with the laws of statics. Mozart, on the other hand, prefers to join together the most wonderful melodic ideas as prefabricated components; observe how in the first movement of K.271 he varies the succession of his building-blocks, to the extent of shaking them up as though in a kaleidoscope. Whereas Beethoven draws one element from another, in what might be called a procedural manner, Mozart arranges one element after another as though it could not be otherwise.

Mozart, more than most other composers, expresses himself differently in minor and in major keys. That he could also compose in a procedural manner is demonstrated by his two concertos in minor keys, K.466 and 491, which so greatly impressed Beethoven. Original cadenzas for these two works unfortunately do not exist. Neither the dynamic spaciousness of the D minor concerto nor the contrapuntal density of the C minor concerto is compatible with the usual type of improvisational cadenza in Mozart's concertos in major keys. Rather more conceivable are cadenzas in the manner of Bach's Fifth Brandenburg Concerto which carry on the intensity of the movement, transporting it in a broad arc to the next entrance of the orchestra.

*

Mozart is made neither of porcelain, nor of marble, nor of sugar. The cute Mozart, the perfumed Mozart, the permanently ecstatic Mozart, the 'touch-me-not' Mozart, the sentimentally bloated Mozart must all be avoided. There should be some slight doubt, too, about a Mozart who is incessantly 'poetic'. 'Poetic' players may find themselves sitting in a hothouse in which no fresh air can enter; you want to come and open the windows. Let poetry be the spice, not the main course. It is significant that there are only 'poets of the keyboard'; a relatively prosaic instrument needs to be transformed, bewitched. Violinists, conductors, even lieder singers – so usage would suggest – seem to survive without 'poetry'.

*

One look at the solo parts of Mozart's piano concertos should be enough to show the Mozart player that his warrant leaves that of a museum curator far behind. Mozart's notation is not complete. Not only do the solo parts lack dynamic markings almost entirely; the very notes to be played – at any rate in the later works that were not made ready for the engraver – require piecing out at times: by filling (when Mozart's manuscript is limited to sketchy indications); by variants (when relatively simple themes return several times without Mozart varying them himself); by embellishments (when the player is entrusted with a melodic outline to decorate); by re-entry fermatas (which are on the dominant and must be connected to the subsequent tonic); and by cadenzas (which lead from the six-four chord in quasi-improvisational fashion to the concluding tutti).

Luckily, there are a good number of Mozart's own variants, embellishments, re-entries and cadenzas, and they give the player a clear idea of his freedom of movement. In re-entries and cadenzas the main key is never deviated from; in embellishments and variants the prevailing character is never disturbed. Mozart's variants sometimes show a subtle economy which, I assume, was not in keeping with contemporary convention.[1] The view that empty spots must stay empty because the performer cannot possibly claim to possess Mozart's genius has been overcome today; it was an attitude produced by misguided reverence, which did not expect or trust the player to have the necessary empathy with Mozart's style. The case of the Rondo in A major K.386 is instructive; thanks to the recent discovery of the last pages of Mozart's manuscript, we now realize that the final twenty-eight bars of the Rondo, as we used to know it, are not by Mozart but by Cipriani Potter, which no one would otherwise have noticed.

It is precisely in those passages where Mozart's text is sketchy that the player must know exactly what Mozart wrote and how he wrote it, and not put his faith in editors. Anyone who takes on Mozart's piano concertos will have to devote some time to studying the sources. A particular case in point is the so-called 'Coronation' Concerto K.537. Most of the left hand is not worked out at all. In the middle movement, which is plagued by a complete lack of emotional contrast, the same four-bar phrase appears no fewer than ten times in virtually identical guise. Here the richest ornamentation will be needed if the effect is not to resemble the pallid charm of certain Raphael Madonnas, which the nineteenth century adored, just as it did this movement, unembellished. It is not at all easy to understand why a version of this lovely work fabricated after Mozart's death is still generally played today, as though nothing about it could stand to be improved.

*

Additions to Mozart's text are in some instances obviously required, in others at least possible. An appendix to the Bärenreiter complete edition prints a lavishly embellished version of the F sharp minor Adagio from the Concerto in A major K.488; it is probably the work of a pupil, and apparently was part of Mozart's musical estate. What is

---

[1] In his C minor Concerto K.491 the extremely delicate shifts of harmony, part-writing and rhythm at the returns of the initial theme should be savoured without further additions.

elaborated in this manuscript is in no way satisfactory, but it does provide a clue that embellishment is permitted. As to how one is to go about it, Mozart's own models, and no others, are the ones to be guided by. The embellishments by Hummel or Philipp Karl Hoffmann do not even try to follow Mozart's example; they are foreign to his style and frequently overcrowded with notes to such a degree that, to get all of them in, the relatively flowing tempi of Mozart's middle movements must be pulled back to largo. The additions by Hummel and Hoffmann do make us aware that the 'gusto' of performance style could change quite quickly and drastically; this should give pause to those who try to get at Mozart by concentrating too single-mindedly on baroque practice.

The player's delight at filling in the white spots on Mozart's musical map in such a way that even the educated listener does not prick up his ears must stay within bounds. The player must not be seduced into overdoing it or into living too much for the moment. When improvising embellishments becomes a parlour game gleefully played to flummox the orchestra, when the player sets out in every performance to prove to himself and all present that he is indeed spontaneous, he is in danger of losing control over quality. I think he will be more deserving if he makes a rigorous selection from a supply of versions he has improvised at home, rather than risking everything on the platform by trying to play Mozart as though he *were* Mozart.

*

One of the additions that is possible but rarely necessary, since in most cases it merely doubles the orchestra, is continuo playing. Once I relished accompanying the bass line of the orchestra, but today I usually limit myself to taking a hand occasionally in energetic passages and to giving almost imperceptible harmonic support to some piano cantilenas. At a time when there were neither conductors nor full scores, the basso continuo, apart from giving the soloist his harmonic bearings, served mainly to co-ordinate the players' rhythm. Nowadays one can reasonably expect the soloist to

be familiar with the score (lately even lieder singers are
expected to have taken a glance at the piano accompaniment); and naturally we expect the conductor to keep the
orchestra together. Basso continuo playing therefore seems
to have a point only in special cases, such as when the four
Mozart chamber concertos (K.413–415 and 449) are performed without winds. But the difference between solo and
tutti must not be lost.

*

Even a composer like Mozart could make a mistake. Artur
Schnabel's precept that the performer must accept the whims
of great composers though he may be quite unable to fathom
them must not be allowed to go so far that errors remain
unrectified. Schnabel himself provided some examples of
reverential blindness, as when, for example, in the middle
movement of the Concerto in C minor K.491, he played a
bar, with wind accompaniment, precisely as Mozart inadvertently let it stand. Here, as in one bar of the finale of K.503,
Mozart apparently wrote the piano part first and then, when
writing in the orchestral parts, changed his mind about the
harmony. In doing so he forgot to adjust the piano part to
the new harmonic situation. The result is cacophony and a
divergence in the leading of the bass line that is unthinkable
in Mozart. If the player, in rare instances, puts Mozart's text
right, it does not mean that he presumes himself to be equal,
or indeed superior, to Mozart.

   With the *alla breve* of the middle movement of K.491,
Mozart seems to set us a riddle, but for once without giving
us 'the solution with the riddle' (to quote another of Busoni's
Mozart aphorisms). Paul and Eva Badura-Skoda have gone
to some lengths to explain why Mozart must have made a
mistake with this marking. In its note values, the movement
is twice as slow as the *alla breve* movements in Concertos
K.466, 537 and 595. As confirmed by the textbooks of the
period, and by Beethoven's metronome figures, the *alla breve*
marking stands not only for counting half-bars but also for a
considerable increase in tempo. Yet there are exceptions, as

Erich Leinsdorf has been kind enough to point out to me,
and the second movement of K.491 is one. Leinsdorf
mentions, among others, some examples from *The Magic
Flute* (Overture: Adagio; No. 8: Larghetto; Act II: March of
the Priests; No. 18: Chorus of the Priests; No. 21: Andante)
where the *alla breve* 'should be translated to a contemporary
conductor meaning: in four, my boy, not in eight'. But there
is also the Aria with gamba 'Es ist vollbracht' ('It is finished')
from Bach's St John Passion where Bach indicated, above the
3/4 of the middle section, the words *alla breve*, suggesting the
'next faster unit': in three, not in six. The old complete
edition, which altered several of Mozart's tempo markings
arbitrarily, transformed the *alla breve* in the first movement
of the Concerto in F major K.459 into 4/4 time, thereby
doing precisely what this piece cannot tolerate: it is meant to
move along not *alla marcia*, as we are constantly told in
commentaries and hear in performances, but dancingly and
in whole bars.

*

Mozart was not a flower child. His rhythm is neither weak
nor vague. Even the tiniest, softest tone has backbone.
Mozart may dream now and then, but his rhythm stays
awake. Let the tempo modifications in Mozart be signs of a
rhythmic strength that counterbalances emotional strength;
above all in variation movements, it will surely be permissible
to graduate the tempo at times, to set off the variations from
one another. Mozart may lament – and that lamentation can
reach a pitch of solitary grief – but he does not moan and
groan. Two-note patterns should be 'sighed' only when the
music really demands sighing. Not only singers should be
aware of the difference between a suspension, which has a
purely musical role, and an appoggiatura, whose role is
emotional and declamatory, stressing the pathos of two-
syllable words.

*

Is Mozart's music simple? For his contemporaries it was
frequently too complicated. The idea of simplicity has

become downright embarrassing in this century. There is a 'kitsch' of plainness, especially noticeable in the literary glorification of the 'simple life' and in a longing for the 'popular vein'. What was all right for the Romantics is thought to be reasonable enough for their descendants. Simplicity in playing Mozart must not mean subjecting diversity to a levelling process or running away from problems. Simplicity is welcome as long as the point is to avoid superfluity. But to 'concentrate only on what counts' in Mozart is questionable. Everything in his music counts, if we leave out a few weaker works or movements, of which there are some even among Mozart's piano concertos, for example the early pieces preceding that wonder of the world, the 'Jeunehomme' Concerto K.271.

The identity of Mlle Jeunehomme seems to remain just as mysterious as the sudden supreme mastery that unfolds in the work composed for her. Here it is revealed for the first time that Mozart is both 'as young as a youth' and 'as wise as an old man' (Busoni). And from this point on, the Mozart player must shoulder a burden of perfection that goes beyond his powers.

*(1985)*

# Must Classical Music be Entirely Serious?

## 1 The Sublime in Reverse

### I

In a remarkable essay on Schubert, Antonín Dvořák[1] makes it clear that he cannot consider Schubert's masses ecclesiastical, even though he concedes that the feeling for what is truly sacred music 'may differ somewhat among nations and individuals', as does the sense of humour.

I own a cartoon from Czechoslovakia. In it a pianist is shown sitting on a concert platform. But instead of performing the piece on the music stand in front of him, he is helpless with laughter. The composition that provokes his amusement bears the title 'A. Dvořák – Humoresk'. In the cartoon the faces of the audience are all completely serious; they appear quite unmoved by the mirth of the pianist, who must surely have been the first to discover that Dvořák's Humoresque should be a matter for laughter. Of course, a pianist's audience is not supposed to laugh, but neither is the pianist.

Humoresques are notoriously unfunny. In the German-speaking countries and Central Europe the word 'humoresque' was applied to a literary genre: a short, good-humoured and amiable story that avoided the grotesque or satirical. Schumann's beautiful Humoresque differs from later ones in being a piece on a much grander scale, in both size and emotional scope; if it aims for a 'felicitous blend of rapture and wit' (to use one of Jean Paul's formulas for humour), what it mainly achieves is to be capricious, lyrical and unpredictable.

---

[1] See p. 80

For those who claim that music cannot be truly comical without the assistance of words, or without relating to visible reality, humoresques from Schumann to Rachmaninov and Reger seem to provide ample proof. So, I am afraid, does Mozart's *A Musical Joke*, usually regarded as a prize example of musical wit. It is a work in which, as far as I can see, a catalogue of musical blunders is distributed with little kindness, along with some blatantly wrong notes that the performers are made to play on purpose.

Where, then, does one look for the comical in music outside the realm of opera and song? There are, of course, pieces with funny titles. 'Ouf! les petits pois' or 'Prélude inoffensif' show that Rossini, in those late compositions that are called *Sins of Old Age*, refused to take himself as seriously as the Romantic composers did. This man, who throughout his life suffered discomfort from several illnesses, kept up the appearance of a musical buffoon; his delightful non-operatic music, unusual in its time, casts no shadows. Some of Rossini's pieces make me laugh even without their titles, whereas nearly all of Erik Satie's melancholy miniatures are funny only on account of their titles.

For me, the most convincingly comical absolute music has been written by the Viennese classical masters and by some twentieth-century composers. György Ligeti's *Aventures et Nouvelles aventures*, even on records, should make almost anybody laugh – and much more so if you *watch* the singers and players produce all those lovely noises in the concert hall. The work qualifies as absolute music because it does not employ words, and it is not basically theatrical. It is reminiscent of human utterance, action and behaviour, which to me remains one of the legitimate effects of music even if, in the past, it used to be achieved in a far more stylized fashion.

I do not know whether the public in Haydn's time ever laughed during, or at the end of, a performance. For perfectly good reasons, there is an understanding between a civilized audience and the performers that the music should be played, and listened to, without too many additional noises. There is no shortage of evidence that at least some of Haydn's and Beethoven's contemporaries had a musical sense of humour, and admired it in the works of the two composers. In one of the most important early essays on Haydn, Ignaz Ernst Ferdinand Arnold[1] made an acute comment on Haydn's comic style:

Being in command of all artistic means, this play of easy imagination endows even the smallest flight of genius with a boldness and audacity [*Keckheit und Dreistigkeit*] that expands the area of aesthetic achievement into the infinite without causing damage or anxiety ... The last Allegros or Rondos consist frequently of short, nimble movements that reach the highest degree of comicality by often being worked out most seriously, diligently and learnedly ... Any pretence at seriousness only serves the purpose of making the playful wantonness of the music appear as unexpected as possible, and of teasing us from every side until we succumb and give up all attempts to predict what will happen next, to ask for what we wish for, or to demand what is reasonable.

According to Georg August Griesinger, an early biographer of Haydn, 'a sort of innocent mischievousness, or what the British call humour, was a principal trait of Haydn's character. He easily discovered what he preferred – the comical side of things.' Haydn himself confessed (to Albert Christoph Dies) that there is a frame of mind in which, to quote Dies, 'a certain kind of humour takes possession of you and cannot be restrained'. He also thought this was a quality which stemmed from an abundance of good health. About Beethoven, Friedrich Rochlitz writes: 'Once Beethoven is in the mood, rough, striking witticisms, odd notions, surprising and exciting juxtapositions and paradoxes occur to him in a steady flow.'[2] If we apply this statement to Beethoven's comic music, we have a valuable list of characteristics that bear musical scrutiny.

---

[1] 'Josef Haydn', *Bildungsbuch für junge Tonkünstler*, Erfurt 1810
[2] *Für Freunde der Tonkunst*, Leipzig 1868, IV, 235

# II

Before I present some musical examples I should like to draw attention to the fact that there is widespread confusion about the meaning of humour, irony and wit. Not only does it differ from language to language; in the sense of Dvořák's remark quoted above, it turns out to be a deeply personal matter, as indeed religion should be. (According to another of Jean Paul's definitions, humour is 'the sublime in reverse' – *das umgekehrte Erhabene*.) I can therefore only submit a choice of pieces that I personally find funny, amusing, ludicrous or hilarious, and I have settled for the word 'comic' to signify an ingredient that is common to all of them. Whether oddities and incongruities of a purely musical nature will strike the listener as hilarious, strange or disturbing must depend on the psychological climate of each piece, but also on the psychological disposition of each listener.

Let me start with a piece by Haydn. Before taking in the complete third movement of Haydn's late C major Sonata Hob. XVI:50, I would ask you to read, or play, through an edited version of it. In the musical text I have indicated where four bars of the first part, and thirty of the second, should be left out.

Comparing the edited and the complete version, I would already call the shorter one a burlesque. The teasing avoidance of classical four- or eight-bar patterns, the abortive storm in D minor that peters out almost before it begins, and its laughing and bouncing staccatos contribute towards making it comical. The complete version of the piece, however, is ludicrous to a much greater degree. By introducing the 'wrong' B major chords as the most memorable surprise, it presents the listener with an intriguing problem. How should we 'understand' these chords? How many explanations can we find for them? And which of these explanations prevails?

The listener's initial impression of the first B major chord must be that of a *faux pas*. When we try to verify this impression we soon get into trouble. How would a player of a C major piece who has stumbled into a B major chord by mistake behave? He could, like Sir Adrian Boult in the first performance of Tippett's Second Symphony, turn to the audience, say 'Sorry, my fault', and start again. More probably, he or she would try to cover up the blunder.

In this way, the offence of the B major chord would be 'rationalized'; a mistake would be turned into an advantage, *Schadenfreude* into admiration for the player's quick reaction. The listener would, ironically speaking, laugh not at the player but *with* him.

The second-best way out for the imaginary player would be to pretend that nothing had happened. Somebody slips on a banana skin and suddenly finds himself sitting on the ground; it will take him a few moments to pick himself up and proceed, *come prima*, with an innocent face. That is what Haydn *seems* to have done. A second hearing, though, may reveal that the 'wrong' B major chord does not come completely out of the blue. The piece that had started, and continues, in purely diatonic writing brings in, as a little warning, a C sharp in the bar before. A C natural here would sound downright harmless, as indeed it is supposed to sound four bars later when the same figure returns.

Is, then, our B major chord a premeditated challenge that is not accepted? After all, Haydn could have stayed within the means of musical propriety and continued in the following fashion:

We know more about the B major chord when it has reappeared in the recapitulation. It reasserts itself, almost menacingly, with the help of a ritardando, after a short digression into C minor has ended on the Neapolitan D flat (bars 58–65). More than anything else, the indicated ritard underlines the fact that this is not simply a reproduction of the 'memory lapse' or 'slip of the tongue' that had occurred earlier. This is not just a mistake obstinately repeating itself. The proximity of the Neapolitan harmony makes the B major chord all the more provocative. Again, there is no apology afterwards; neither is there any sign of unease. The piece continues in high spirits, laughing at us at the end.

I am aware that there is some sort of harmonic resolution to the B major irritant four bars later. In the recapitulation (69, 73) it is resolved into the dominant seventh. As I feel it, these cheerful resolutions do not calm the psychological seas completely. They do not, and should not, remove the final suspicion that these B major chords are arbitrary and unjustified, an insult veiled by apparent innocence, an act of splendid nonsense that is all the more delightful because it cannot be explained away. As Schopenhauer said in his analysis of laughter: 'It is diverting to see the strict, untiring, troublesome governess, Reason, for once convicted of inadequacy.'

Summing up the comic traits in Haydn's piece, I find: (1) breaches of convention; (2) the appearance of ambiguity; (3) proceedings that masquerade as something they are not, for instance as lacking professional knowledge or skill; (4) veiled insults; and (5) nonsense. All of these distinctions belong to the stock-in-trade of the comical in general.[1]

A comic feature that is specific to music is the evocation of laughing and leaping, familiar manifestations of playfulness and high spirits that can be musically suggested by short staccato, leaps of large intervals, and short groups of fast notes separated by rests, as in the scherzos of two A major sonatas: Beethoven's Op. 2 No. 2 and Schubert's D.959. In Kandinsky's late painting *Scherzklänge* (Jocular Sounds), such musical effects become visible by means of abstract art: short staccato is represented by wedges, while hopping or skipping is suggested by arched shapes. Though musical laughing and leaping may not be sufficient to make a piece of music comical, it can greatly contribute towards setting a mood from which comic surprise will emerge.

# III

To become apparent, breaches of order need a framework of order. In other comical contexts, the framework is given by words and their meaning, by human situations and reactions, and by the kind of thought that is connected with language. In music, the framework relies on the established musical

---

[1] I am especially indebted to D.H. Munro's survey of comical tendencies in his book *Argument of Laughter*, Melbourne University Press, 1951.

forms and expectations, and on the logic of purely musical thought. Such a framework is indeed available to the musical layman; the musical experience that is needed is comparable to the verbal experience a child needs to understand a joke. Of course, there are also sophisticated jokes for grown-ups.

Why does classical music lend itself so readily to comic effects? Because it seems to me to reflect, in its solid and self-sufficient forms and structures, the trust of the Enlightenment in rational structures that rule the universe.[1] The spirit of classical music seems to imply the belief that the world is good, or at least that it could become so. For the Romantics, there was no sense of order to rely upon; it had to be found and created in oneself. The open and fragmentary structures of romantic music, as epitomized by the fantasy, aimed to be as personal, and exceptional, as possible. Where, as with Berlioz, surprise becomes the governing principle of composition, and music a succession of feverish dreams, comic effects have little chance; they have to be achieved as an assault on what is proper and predictable.

Cadenzas of classical concertos were allowed, and supposed, to be unpredictable. The final trill, however, traditionally leading from the dominant seventh into the tonic and the orchestral tutti, was something that could be relied on, for listeners and orchestral players alike. Beethoven, one of the supreme musical architects, wrote cadenzas that make Mozart's look like models of restraint. In the marathon cadenza for his own C major Concerto, the trill is the special target of his mockery. It never happens as it should. After some hundred bars that run amok through various keys and wreck classical conventions right and left, the cadenza appears to come to an end. The dominant of C major is reached, the trill has begun. But why has there been a diminuendo that deflated the tension? And why is there no

---

[1] 'A sense of humour develops in a society to the degree that its members are simultaneously conscious of being each a unique person and of being all in common subjection to unalterable laws.' W.H. Auden, 'Notes on the Comic' in *The Dyer's Hand* (Faber, 1963)

dominant seventh chord? If this was to be the proper conclusion, the situation has been mishandled.

Again, we are in an area of ambiguity. We may have the impression of heroic bravura running out of steam; but also of turning in a new, poetic direction indicated by a trill that is not brilliant but lyrical. For a moment, time stands still. What is the composer going to do? Nothing happens that we expect.

We have been plunged, rather cruelly, from a 'higher emotional level' to a 'lower' one. Instead of a lyrical episode, or an orchestral tutti, we get a parody of the third theme in G major, a key that sounds provocatively out of place because Beethoven did not modulate there. Soon the unreality of the harmonic situation makes room for the harmony we were missing; throughout the considerable remainder of the cadenza, the presence of the dominant seventh remains unchallenged. Another ironic attempt at a final trill proves useless because the chord is in the wrong position (that of the second):

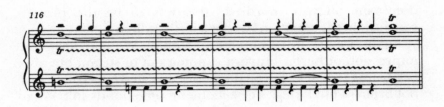

Ultimately, when the dominant seventh has been let loose in a frenzy of vehemently repeated scales, there is a last, truly bizarre surprise: the two final chords are, 'unnecessarily', interrupted by a soft, short, arpeggiated one. Playing the end of the cadenza without this soft chord and leading directly into the orchestral tutti helps us to realize the degree of Beethoven's mischief.

If this chord could speak an aside to the public, or the orchestra, we might well make out something like: 'Are we really coming to an end?', 'Wouldn't you like the cadenza to be over?', 'What a ridiculous frenzy!', 'Heavens, didn't we forget the trill?', 'As it didn't work before, why should it work now?', or simply 'Am I fooling you well?'

# IV

Comic irreverence in classical music has a rational and an irrational significance. The rational side may be illuminated by a quotation from Francis Hutcheson: 'Nothing is so properly applied to the false Grandeur, either of Good or of Evil, as ridicule.' And, according to Schiller, the comic writer has 'continuously to amuse reason', 'shun pathos' and 'defend himself against passions'. Comic music has no other use for the solemn, the rapturous, the pastoral, the heroic or the frenzied than to make fun of it. On the other hand, irrationalism, which had started to undermine the 'certainties' of reason, is musically manifest as a mockery of what is normal, worthy and well-behaved. What rationalism does to grand emotions, irrationalism does to the civilized procedures of musical form. Diderot likened great artists, in their defiance of rules, to great criminals, and he conceded that the dark forces in man had their share in the creation of works of art. Nowhere have these dark forces surfaced more cheerfully than in several of Haydn's finales, and more disquietingly than in some of his works in minor keys.

It needs to be said that any formal peculiarities are not sufficient evidence for the comic leanings of a piece. Form and psychology have to interact. Two hallmarks of Haydn's eccentricity, his sudden rests and fermatas at unlikely places, and his extended repetitions of the same soft chord, or note, over several bars, can have a very different psychological impact on the listener in pieces of different character. To suspend, interrupt or freeze the flow of music can be purely hilarious, or purely disturbing. If it is both at once, or oscillates between the two, the effect may be called grotesque. (Ligeti's *Aventures et Nouvelles aventures* is grotesque music, and so is much of the comic music of this century.) Generally, the same devices that make music amusing can also make it strange, eerie, disturbing and macabre. The psychological climate of a piece will finally decide whether they are one or the other, or both. In classical music, they are likely to be one

*or* the other. Incidentally, the colloquial use of the word
'funny' takes care of both the comical and the strange.

The basic key of a basically comic piece is a major key.
There is, outside the field of opera or song, only one comical
example in a minor key that comes to mind: Beethoven's C
minor Bagatelle from Op. 119. The piece is comical because
a cheerful dance that should be in a major key is used to
express grim resolution. Communication of comic resolution
or comic anger is generally reserved for episodes in Beethoven's earlier rondo movements. A well-known example is
the A minor section in his C major Piano Concerto.

This seems a good moment to introduce another area of
comic music: that of the excessive and obsessive, of overstate-
ment and *idée fixe*. There is an 'as if' character about such
music. It may resemble comic acting, caricature and *opera
buffa*. The composer seems to imply: 'This is not really me. I
am just turning into somebody choleric or absent-minded,
into a pedant, a naughty child, or a very, very innocent child,
to amuse you.'

At the beginning of Beethoven's Variations Op. 35 there
is a juxtaposition of excessive contrast: pianissimo and
fortissimo.

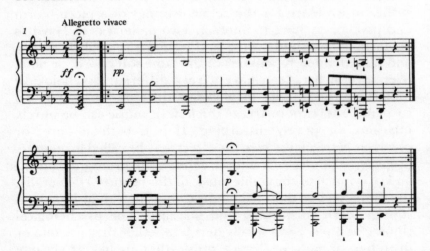

One may call it an alternation of whispering and stentorian

laughter, or of tiptoeing and stamping. Other comic elements are in evidence: the bass alone pretending to be the complete theme (that in effect is only presented later); the rests before and after the fortissimo B flats; and the following B flat, marked *piano*, that appears to me like an actor putting a finger to his lips, and going 'shhhh'.

In the course of these variations, Beethoven plays with the contrast of soft and loud, of changing and repeated notes. In Variation 1 he makes fun of the loud strokes, brings them in too soon, and thereafter cunningly subdues the middle section. In Variations 9 and 13 the loud B flats take over the whole variation as furious grunts, or tear it apart as hysterical shrieks. In Variation 7 there is a series of grim belly-laughs in the bass register, while the rest of the piece is provided with odd accents.

Odd, misplaced, bizarre, obsessive accents are another tool of the composer in a comic frame of mind. The rondo of Beethoven's Second Piano Concerto starts with accents against the grain which later, before the coda, are misplaced in a parody.

The alternation of fast and slow can also generate results of a comical, and highly theatrical, kind, like two different characters who speak *to* one another, or *past* one another. In Variation 21 of Beethoven's Diabelli Variations the utterances of the two characters, one coarsely energetic, the other whining, remain incompatible, and the unity of musical context is startlingly broken up. Before the end of Beethoven's G major Sonata Op. 31 No. 1 there is a succession of different tempi, with adagios almost too slow, and rests almost too long, for comfort – only to be followed by a presto that tries to make up for the wasted thirty seconds by comic haste. The pianist who has not succeeded in making somebody in his audience laugh at the end of this sonata should become an organist.

The sarcastic Hans von Bülow once shouted to a female pupil who tried to play the third movement of Beethoven's 'Lebewohl' ('Les adieux') Sonata: 'Stop! In the joy of reunion, you rush off, get entangled in the train of your dress, crash

down, and smash all the flowerpots in the garden!'[1] I think
certain classical pieces should communicate a whiff of such a
state of mind, with the player in ironic command. Musicians
like Bruno Walter, Edwin Fischer and Artur Schnabel had
more courage to turn such movements into an exhilarating
romp than most of us today.

One of the pieces that can only be appreciated in terms of
the obsessively comical is the first movement of Beethoven's
Sonata Op. 31 No. 1.

If one looks at this piece from a purely formal perspective,
and without any psychological insight, one might dismiss it as
incompetent, repetitious and unworthy of Beethoven. It
would, however, be naïve to assume that Beethoven, in the
course of this movement, brought in the same opening idea
seven times in the same G major, and in an identical position,
without doing so on purpose.

There are further clues to his comic intentions: the two
hands that seem unable to play together; the short staccato;
the somewhat bizarre regularity of brief spells of sound
interrupted by rests. The character that emerges is one of
compulsive, but scatterbrained, determination. The piece
seems unable to go anywhere except where it should not.

---

[1] Theodor Pfeiffer: *Studien bei Hans von Bülow*, Berlin 1894, p. 55

What a nice surprise to find oneself, at the start of the second theme, in B major instead of the dominant, or in E major instead of the tonic; a surprise that, within a sonata form in a major key, must have been a novelty of an almost exotic flavour. Only Beethoven's String Quintet Op. 29 had made use of the mediant – the related third – before, but in its exposition alone. What, in Op. 31 No. 1, sounds jocular and provocative must have signalled to some of Beethoven's contemporaries a delicious disregard of rules, while simply bewildering others. (It took Beethoven's later 'Waldstein' Sonata, as Tovey has pointed out, to establish the same harmonic progressions as a natural part of widely extended harmonic perspectives.) The coda indicates to anybody who may have missed the point that nothing in this piece was meant to be taken at face value.

As for the second movement, Adagio grazioso, here is a version of the theme that I have simplified to make it unfunny.

And here is Beethoven's own version.

I think, of the two versions, Beethoven's original sounds like a parody of early Beethoven produced by Rossini — who, when this sonata was completed, was ten years old. In Beethoven's Adagio, a complicated balance is achieved between sympathy and mockery, the graceful and the bizarre, nostalgia and anticipation, lyricism and irony. What is Beethoven being ironic about? His own style of the early rondos? The manner of coloratura embellishment? The demeanour of a prima donna on stage? Or the slightly grotesque suppleness of a Taglioni or Fanny Elssler, indicated by the well-oiled mechanism of trills, staccato quavers and musical pirouettes? One might call this movement the first neoclassical piece of music. It is an irony in itself that Op. 31 No. 1 seems to have been the only Beethoven sonata Stravinsky did not enjoy.

# V

The combination of incongruous elements is generally regarded as a distinguishing feature of wit. In another example of musical wit, Beethoven's F major finale from the Sonata Op. 10 No. 2, the solemn technique of fugal writing is 'abused' for burlesque purposes.

Adolf Bernhard Marx likened the movement to 'a child that plucks an old man's beard'. Of course, there is never a serious attempt to present a proper fugal exposition and the listener is left wondering what the composer's intentions were, wittily torn between counterpoint and homophony, sonata and rondo, bristling energy and musical laughter. Already Haydn had been commended (by Griesinger) for his ability 'to lure the listener into the highest degree of the comical by frivolous twists and turns of the seemingly serious'. Devices of musical style that were supposed to suggest such elevated emotional states as 'magnanimity, majesty, splendour, rage, revenge, despair, devotion, delight or virtuousness' (to quote from C.P.E. Bach's friend Christian Gottfried Krause, whose book *Von der musikalischen Poesie* impressed Lessing) were applied by Haydn to the lowest category of poetics, the comical. The 'mescolanza di tutti generi' of which Salieri spoke in connection with Haydn's masses is evident also in his comic music. There is a strong

theatrical element in some of Haydn's works, not surprising
in a composer who over a period of fifteen years organized
performances of opera at Eszterháza, and was acquainted
with all comical genres of the musical theatre, marionette
opera included. Haydn himself turned his incidental music
to Jean-François Regnard's *Le distrait* into a capriciously
humorous symphony in six movements known as 'Il distrat-
to'. The success of this symphony shows how fluid the
borderlines were, how readily such music was appreciated
without the stage, and how eagerly the contemporary public,
particularly in France, tried to find out what music 'expresses' or 'represents'.

The promotion of the comical in string quartet, sonata and
symphony is one of Haydn's great innovations. Carl Friedrich Zelter explains in a letter to his friend Goethe (9 March
1814) that Haydn's art was criticized in earlier years
'because', as he says, 'it immediately made a burlesque of the
deadly seriousness of his predecessors', J.S. Bach and C.P.E.
Bach. Haydn certainly did not set out to parody C.P.E. Bach,
whom he revered,[1] in the way early *opéra comique* had
parodied some works of Lully. Rather, the listener was
stimulated to take the comical more seriously, and accept it as
part of one's own life. The term 'the elevated comical' (*das
hohe Komische*) had been used, and may have been coined, to
characterize Haydn's music, including even, as the *Musical
Almanac of 1782* states, the Adagios, 'during which people
actually, and properly, are supposed to weep'.

Beethoven's F major finale from Op. 10 No. 2 starts with
what one may call a 'laughing theme', and the dominating
impact of the movement remains that of laughter. (Nobody
seems to doubt that music can 'sigh', metaphorically speak-

---

[1] From C.P.E. Bach, Haydn adopted not only some exemplary qualities of the early
sonatas ('clear formal disposition, unity of emotion and thematic material in each
movement, consequent motivic development', in the words of the German keyboard
player and scholar Andreas Staier) but also the inclination to be unpredictable. If
C.P.E. Bach, in the 'bizarrerie' that was to become characteristic of his style, ever
tried his hand at suggesting the comical, he was bound to fail. With surprise as the
governing principle, humour could not be accommodated – a situation later
repeated in Berlioz.

ing, but I have read denials that music can 'laugh'.) To some people, the noise of laughter is contagious. To the depressive, laughter may be painful and unavailable. To others, laughter is vulgar, seriousness a sign of maturity, and everything that is hilarious a desecration of loftier states of mind. To step down from one's elevated platform would mean to lose one's self-respect.

The Austrian Emperor Joseph II disapproved of what he called 'Haydn's jests'. Laughter poses a danger to state and religion. Plato wanted to ban it. Laughter is incompatible with the holy and the absolute. Or rather, it is the privilege of the Deity, whether sardonic (as in Indian mythology, and the *Iliad*) or serene (as in Hegel's 'unquenchable laughter of the Gods'). Umberto Eco, dealing with the significance of laughter in his novel *The Name of the Rose*, quotes Pliny the Younger: 'Aliquando praeterea rideo, ioco, ludo, homo sum' ('Sometimes I laugh, I joke, I play, I am human'). The laughter of man is not the laughter of gods. Anybody who has witnessed a little child recognizing a parent, revelling in a new toy, or embarking on an exciting adventure, knows that there is laughter that does not originate in catastrophe, or represent superiority.

In a German musical encyclopaedia of 1875[1] I found an admirable article on humour (the *New Grove* has none); it sets humour apart from other modes of the comical in that it is a world view, a complete outlook on life. 'For the humorist,' the article says, 'there are no fools, only foolishness and a mad world.' (This, again, is a formula borrowed from Jean Paul.) 'He will therefore perceive man and the world to be not ridiculous or revolting but pitiable.' Humour relates to the dark undercurrent of life, and prevails over it. If we understand humour in this comprehensive sense, Beethoven's Diabelli Variations are one of its musical paradigms.

---

[1] *Musikalisches Conversations-Lexikon* (Verlag R. Oppenheim)

# VI

You may have noticed that the name Mozart has hardly been mentioned. In looking for examples in his works, I found myself to be the victim of prejudice. I wrongly assumed that his absolute music should be a mine of the comical because his letters abound in hilarious word-play and nonsense and because the music of his operas makes such superlative use of all comical resources. Haydn and Beethoven, with all their love of cantabile, were predominantly instrumental composers; sensual beauty of sound was not an innate quality, or a primary concern. The imagination of Mozart or Schubert, however, was predominantly vocal, even in their instrumental works, and the style of Mozart's symphonies had been castigated accordingly by Nägeli as too operatic. Singing, like sensuality, is hardly funny. It constitutes an area of beauty that opens itself to the comical only by means of words and comic acting. Singing itself can become comical where it turns into grotesque utterance; the music of our time has seized upon such sounds or noises, suggestive of the absurd and the crudely physical.

Mozart's beauty of cantabile is matched by the beauty of his musical proportion and balance, that singular illusion of complete formal perfection at any time. Next to Mozart's truly classical sense of order, Haydn often appears whimsical. Where Mozart somehow manages to surprise us with what we expect, Haydn excels in the unexpected. The sudden fortissimo chord in the Adagio of his 'Surprise' Symphony is only one of many examples.

Writing about 'The Comical in Music', Schumann claims that Beethoven and Schubert were able to translate any state of mind into music. 'In certain *Moments musicaux*,' so he says, 'I imagine I recognize unpaid tailor's bills.' This would undoubtedly have come as a surprise to Schubert who, according to Eduard Bauernfeld, asked a certain Josef Dessauer whether he knew any funny music when Dessauer pronounced one of Schubert's songs to be too melancholy.

Whatever 'lustig' may have meant to Schubert, his music bears out the fact that it hardly aspires to be comical. Schumann's sometimes does; of the important Romantic composers, he was the only one to be influenced by those German Romantic writers to whom humour and irony were a major concern. But Schumann's 'Humor', wherever indicated in his music, is too good-humoured and warmly lyrical to be comic, and his capriciousness does not come from a light-hearted disposition. I cannot find a trace of humour in the music of Chopin, or Liszt. And Wagner is reported to have turned Schiller's line 'Ernst ist das Leben, heiter die Kunst' on its head: art must be serious, while life may be cheerful. The only excuse for the Romantic composer to write funny music seems to have been the use of a funny text, in opera or song.

For most performers and virtually all concert audiences of our time, music is an entirely serious business. Performers are meant to function as heroes, dictators, poets, seducers, magicians, or helpless vessels of inspiration. The projection of comical music needs a performer who dares to be less than awe-inspiring, and does not take him- or herself too seriously. Comic music can be ruined, and made completely meaningless, by 'serious' performance. It is much more dependent on a performer's understanding than an Allegro di bravura, a nocturne, or a funeral march. To manage to play a piece humorously is a special gift, yet, I am afraid, it is not enough: the public, expecting the celebration of religious rites, may not notice that something amusing is going on unless it is visibly encouraged to be amused.

I admit that to expect a player to radiate amusement while performing is a tall order. The trouble is that many performers, on account of their concentration and nervous tension, look unduly grave or grim, no matter what they play. The first bars of a classical piece set its mood. To sit down and start Haydn's last C major Sonata with a tortured look is even worse than to embark on the so-called 'Moonlight' Sonata with a cheerful smile. Nobody will mistake the first movement of the 'Moonlight' for a cheerful piece, whereas the hilarious beginning of Haydn's C major Sonata can easily sound wooden, and pointless. Before the first note, a discreet signal has to pass from the performer to the audience: 'Caution! We are out for mischief.'

When the English notion of 'humour' arrived in Germany, Lessing translated it as 'Laune'. *Laune*, according to Kant, means, in its best sense, 'the talent voluntarily to put oneself into a certain mental disposition, in which everything is judged quite differently from the ordinary method (reversed, in fact), and yet in accordance with certain rational principles in such a frame of mind'. This sounds to me like an apt description of the quality that a performer of comical music should be able to summon up. 'But this manner,' as Kant further says, 'belongs rather to pleasant than to beautiful art, because the object of the latter must always show a certain dignity in itself . . .'[1]

For my part, I am perfectly happy to enjoy the 'sublime in reverse', and leave Kant's dignity behind where Haydn and Beethoven took such obvious pleasure in doing so.

*(1984)*

---

[1] Immanuel Kant: *Critique of Judgment* (1790) § 54

# Must Classical Music be Entirely Serious?

## 2  Beethoven's Diabelli Variations

### I

Despite their vast range of different emotions, serious, lyrical, mysterious and depressive, withdrawn and brilliantly extroverted, Beethoven's Diabelli Variations reveal themselves to be a humorous work in the widest possible sense. Beethoven's first biographer, Anton Schindler, says – and for once I am inclined to believe him – that the composition of this work 'amused Beethoven to a rare degree', that it was written 'in a rosy mood', and that it was 'bubbling with unusual humour', disproving the belief that Beethoven spent his late years in complete gloom. According to Wilhelm von Lenz, one of the most perceptive early commentators on Beethoven's music, Beethoven here shines as the 'most thoroughly initiated high priest of humour'; he calls the variations 'a satire on their theme'.

The theme itself – which Diabelli had sent to fifty fellow composers, asking them to contribute one variation each – is comical because both halves are so stubbornly alike, and because it seems to be trying to be something it is not. It is not a genuine waltz of any kind. If one disregards the dynamic markings and tempo indication *vivace*, it rather resembles an old-fashioned minuet. With its markings, on the other hand, the piece tries a bit too hard to mimic a modern bagatelle; indeed, Konrad Wolff has asked whether all these thoroughly un-Diabellian crescendos and sforzandos might not be additions by Beethoven himself.

Compared with any of Beethoven's previous variation works, the Diabelli Variations are highly unorthodox. An unwritten rule of classical variation practice stipulated that the first variation should remain close to the character of the theme. Beethoven counters such expectations, and the unreality of the 'waltz', immediately with a march. (In his splendid monograph on the Diabelli Variations, William Kinderman[1] has shown that this was an afterthought; while the majority of the pieces were composed in 1819, the march is one of ten variations added by Beethoven after the completion of his last three sonatas, and the *Missa solemnis*, in 1822.) Later in the set, at least eight of the variations laugh or giggle; some others take on an air of the grotesque, of diablerie – if the pun is permitted.

But apart from its sense of comedy, there is relatively little in the theme that informs the set as a whole. The theme has ceased to reign over its unruly offspring. Rather, the variations decide what the theme may have to offer them. Instead of being confirmed, adorned and glorified, it is improved, parodied, ridiculed, disclaimed, transfigured, mourned, stamped out, and finally uplifted.

Even the more innovative of Beethoven's sets had adhered to some 'classical' component as a matter of principle: the Prometheus Variations Op. 35 to the bass, the Op. 34 set to the melody. In the Diabelli Variations the components Beethoven makes use of are variable, and a matter of choice. Some variations are dominated by one motif while leaving others in the background: variations 2, 6, 9, 11, 12 and 25 employ the initial embellishment figure, variations 7 and 19 the broken chord, variations 27 and 28 the sequential motif of bars 9–12 of the theme. In their unprecedented freedom of choice, the Diabelli Variations always retain enough of the motivic material to make their connection with the theme sufficiently clear. As in Beethoven's sonatas, the motivic components of the opening theme are more important than the theme itself in providing the unifying threads for the whole work.

If there is one feature of the theme that is most

---

[1] Clarendon Press, Oxford, 1987

consistently honoured, if modified and refined, it is its build-up of foreshortenings in both halves. Otherwise, the basic design is often called in question. Even its phrase lengths are frequently ignored: no fewer than ten variations shorten or augment its layout, or change its proportions (not to mention the fugue, and those variations in which some or all repeats are missing for good reason).

Apart from the urge to make fun of the theme, there is another evident explanation for such liberties. In a work of this unique size and scope, the listener who remains exposed to the key of C major (and, very sparingly, C minor) for little less than an hour needs to be stimulated in novel ways. In addition to the unending variety of texture and temperament there is the variation of the formal scheme itself.

Only the fugue in E flat (Variation 32) leaves the home key. It calls to mind Handel's lapidary style, but it also conceals the maximum aggressive tension. In its almost boundless energy, it presents an example of what must have been Beethoven's most personal contribution to contrapuntal writing: the explosive fugue. Not that Beethoven, as is so often assumed, had to wrestle desperately with the fugal idiom. This notion has already been gloriously refuted earlier on in the Fughetta (Variation 24), a piece of other-worldly purity, and one of those few variations in the set that reach into the mysterious and sublime. (If humour, according to Jean Paul, is 'the sublime in reverse', then variations such as Nos. 14, 20 and 24 offer the contrast of sublimity in full view.)

Three variations in C minor (Nos. 29–31) prepare the ground for the fugal eruption. The third of these elegies combines again the old and the new: a Bachian aria fused with almost Chopinesque figuration. The closing variation begins as a tribute to Mozart. From a distance of thirty-three variations, its 'tempo di minuetto' lifts the mask from the original theme with irony and affection. What had started out as a satire ends as a work of humour in Jean Paul's comprehensive sense.

# II

To my mind, it has not been sufficiently stressed that Beethoven's greatest set of variations leaves a good many conventions of classical variation practice behind. In his title Beethoven uses the German word 'Veränderungen' (alterations, rather than variations), although elsewhere in the work he adheres to the standard Italian terminology. The boldest of these alterations are structural. 'To interpolate a digression, or to alter the phrase-lengths of a variation, is to incur a risk which the great masters of classical variation form hardly ever venture,' says Tovey. It is a pity that Tovey did not pursue this train of thought any further, instead of asking himself whether Beethoven, in two or three variations, might not have 'inadvertently omitted a bar'.[1]

Let me give you a survey of those variations which shorten, or extend, the theme, or change its organization. In the first half of Var. 4, and the second of Var. 11, one bar is missing where, almost imperceptibly, two phrases are pushed into one another. In Var. 21 there is an excess of eight (4+4) bars, to comical effect. Var. 22 parodies the theme with the help of 'Notte e giorno faticar' from the beginning of Mozart's *Don Giovanni*. Two bars are added to give Leporello[2] the chance to find his way back into C major, whereas the 'German dance' of Var. 25 feigns incompetence by 'losing' the last bar of its first half.

In Var. 29 there are a couple of excess bars in each half:

---

[1] Donald Francis Tovey: *Beethoven* (Oxford, 1944) pp. 125, 129; *The Forms of Music* (Oxford, 1944) p. 244
[2] It has been said that Beethoven's relationship to his theme, like Leporello's relationship to his master, was critical but faithful. To me, a classical borderline of faithfulness has been overstepped.

Without these bars, the structure of the variation falls into place if we understand that every two bars of the theme correspond with one of the variation. No. 30 repeats its last four bars only. Var. 31 compresses the first eight bars of the theme into two, whereafter its foreshortenings take their own time, multiplying their coloratura of grief. We encounter irregular halves of six and five bars respectively in which each last bar consists of twelve quavers instead of nine.

While some of these 'deformations' easily escape notice, anomalies such as missing repeats are quite obvious, if less significant. In other works by Beethoven, the occasional irregular repeat always expands the structure, adding repeats where the theme had none. This has never been deemed offensive, whereas the breaking of pattern in the Diabelli Variations by infrequently leaving out repeats indicated by the theme has irked some musicians, who feel cheated in their most basic expectations of proportion. (Artur Schnabel, in his celebrated recording, repeated the first half of Var. 2, contrary to Beethoven's intention.) Beethoven's priority here is psychological, not formal: where repeats are missing, he counteracts monotony in variations which are based on short, recurring rhythmic figures and contain little rhythmic variety. Vars. 2, 11 and 12 offer no first-part repeat. Vars. 20 and 29 skip both repeats, suggesting intense concentration. In Var. 30 a sighing coda of desolation is created by repeating the final four bars only. But why, it has been asked, did Beethoven not proceed similarly in those other variations which are also steeped in one short rhythmic idea? Let me submit my answers. In Vars. 1 and 9 the insistence on recurring patterns is comical, a stubborn demonstration of muscular power. In Var. 25 the missing bar has to be verified: one needs to hear it missing twice to believe what the player has done. In Var. 26 the very wide compass of pitch makes up for the rhythmic uniformity of semiquavers. Var. 28, again, is obsessed with its own manic energy, a paroxysm of comic rage or laughter.

# III

It is interesting that those 'un-Diabellian' crescendos mentioned by Konrad Wolff remain the single element of Diabelli's theme that Beethoven discards. (Which shows that he could not have inserted them in the first place.) They are not structural enough to be of any strictly musical value. Yet Beethoven takes up their psychological cue – the licence to proceed grotesquely in his own structural way. If the ludicrous, drastic and weird juxtaposition of highly disparate elements is characteristic of the grotesque, then the Diabelli Variations are a remarkably grotesque work. From Var. 13 on, the set offers an almost unbroken succession of sharply defined contrasts. Nothing seems to be more indicative of the prevailing comical spirit than the fact that the most sublime seriousness in Vars. 14, 20 and 24 is immediately followed by light comedy, or farce. The suddenness, on the other hand, with which the depressive minor key sphere takes hold of the piece after the frenzy of Var. 28 recalls an unforgettable visual image from Alain Resnais' *Last Year in Marienbad*: a bedroom is shown in whiter and whiter light until its whiteness gives way, within an instant, to the near-black view of the garden.

For grotesque surprises *within* variations, examples abound. Let me pick out three. In Var. 13 short bites of sound are startlingly juxtaposed with silence. Var. 15 jumps into the bass in bar 22, confounding anybody who looks for amiable logic and euphony, yet making, to my ears, a great deal more sense than the 'corrections' attempted since Moscheles. Var. 21 breaks up the unity of each half by splitting it into two different metres, paces and characters.

# IV

Another overstepped borderline is exemplified by the much-discussed mysterious Var. 20. The enigmatic harmo-

nies of bars 9–12 are 'fairly easily explainable', or so Hans
von Bülow believed.

To me, Bülow's explanations, or anybody else's, illuminate
little except the fact that Beethoven commentators wanted
Beethoven's music to remain explicable. (If there is any
logical clue to this passage we shall find it in its motivic
organization; Jürgen Uhde[1] speaks of 'frozen motifs contained in a crystal'.) I cannot see why this mysterious passage
should not have been so conceived as to remain mysterious
for ever. Liszt must have had this passage in mind when he
called the variation 'Sphinx'. Like Haydn's B major chords in
the finale of his C major Sonata Hob. XVI:50, these
harmonies are musically unreasonable. But their effect could
not be more different. By misbehaving, Haydn provokes the
listener's sense of humour. What Beethoven provokes is our
sense of awe.

Among all the twenty-odd contrasts following one another,
that of Vars. 20/21 must be the most striking; it sets hypnotic
introspection against vaudeville. Kinderman sees in Vars.
19–21 a group that shares canonic features as well as the
structural opposition of its halves. I would, nevertheless,
plead for a separation of Vars. 20 and 21 in performance. As
the centrepiece of the Diabelli Variations, its inner sanctum,
Var. 20 also marks the mid-point of their duration. A
moment of silence, to savour the sublime, seems appropriate.

[1] *Beethovens Klaviermusik* (Reclam, 1968), Vol. I, p.542

# V

As Tovey says, Beethoven 'could not have made an enormous set of variations out of the sublime themes which he treats in variation form in his sonata works. Diabelli's theme is as prosaic as the hard-shell businessman who wrote it, but it does mean business ... It is a theme which sets the composer free to build recognizable variations in every conceivable way.'

Thanks to the variety of the material and the clarity of its presentation, Beethoven was propelled to extend his task beyond measure. Allegedly, Beethoven asked Diabelli[1] (who came to urge him finally to deliver the promised variation for Diabelli's volume): 'How many contributions have you got?' 'Thirty-two,' replied Diabelli. 'Go ahead and publish them,' said Beethoven, 'I shall write thirty-three all by myself.' In Beethoven's own pianistic output, the figures 32 and 33 have their special significance: 32 sonatas are followed by 33 variations as a crowning achievement, of which Var. 33 relates directly to the thirty-second sonata's final Adagio.[2] Looking back at Beethoven's outstanding independent variation works, one could point out yet another, playful reason for the composer to have been attracted by the figure 33. There happens to be, between the 32 Variations in C minor and the sets Opp. 34 and 35, a numerical gap. The Diabelli Variations fill it.

Of course, Beethoven must have been perfectly well aware of the musical components entrusted to him by Diabelli. Here is my list of the *motivic elements* offered by the theme:

---

[1] According to Beethoven's friend Karl Holz, who related the story to Lenz (see Wilhelm von Lenz, *Kritischer Katalog sämmtlicher Werke L. van Beethovens*, Vierter Teil, p. 138)

[2] See Michel Butor: *Dialogue avec 33 variations de L. van Beethoven sur une valse de Diabelli* (Gallimard, 1971) pp. 33 ff., and Kinderman, p. 118

1. The upbeat embellishment, changing note, or appoggiatura;

2. The interval of the fourth and fifth;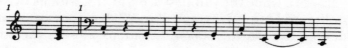

3. The repetitions of single notes or chords, as well as the pedal point (usually on the dominant G);

4. The broken chord (in bars 1–4, 5–8, etc., right hand and left hand);

5. The dance rhythm and its variants;

6. The sequential figure;

7. The melodic curve in the last four bars of each half.

In addition, two *structural elements* should not be overlooked: the series of *foreshortenings* in both halves; and the *melodic direction*, with descending intervals, or motion, in the first half, and ascending ones at the start of the second half. (Diabelli's theme starts its first half with descending fourths and fifths, its second half with an ascending fifth.)

While Beethoven's use of motivic components is capricious, the two structural features mentioned above have, on the whole, earned Beethoven's respect – with the exception of four variations in which motivic or melodic direction as defined above is ignored, namely Vars. 12 (which also makes its foreshortenings almost imperceptible), 22, 28 and 29. In

Var. 18 the descent is maintained in the relation of bars 1
and 3, 5 and 7; the ascent in bars 17 and 19, 21 and 23. In
Fughetta and Fugue, the (main) theme enters alternately
with a fourth and a fifth.

One more element which I have listed among the motivic
components has its structural implications. It is the tone
repetition (or pedal point) on G, spread out over the first
eight bars of both halves: in the melody of bars 1–8, and the
middle voice of bars 17–24. It acts as a spine holding the
harmonies together, particularly emphasized in the repetitions of Vars. 1, 10, 15, 16 and 21, or contained as a latent
idea in the background in Vars. 12 or 26. Of the variations
that depart from this component of the theme, the most
discreet is Var. 8 (bars 5–8), the most demonstrative Var. 9
(bars 16–24), while the funniest are Var. 13, with its (wrong)
beginnings to both halves, and Var. 22 that goes astray after
the double bar. In the *minore* variations 29–31, the structure of the theme disintegrates, and harmonic emphasis
is gradually shifted further and further away from the
dominant.

Another element that is carried into many variations is
what I should like to call a spirit of dance. The theme itself is
a dance, if not clearly a waltz; its initial left-hand rhythm
leaves its mark on at least sixteen of the variations. Some of
them are touched by it only indirectly; in Var. 26 the
continuous semiquaver motion needs the underlying dance
rhythm to come alive.

The turning of this 3/8 variation into a 2/8 triplet piece I can
only take as a misunderstanding.

# VI

Beethoven's humorous variation works are triggered by 'funny' themes. (To my mind, they include not only his Variations Op. 35 and the 'Kind, willst du ruhig schlafen' set, but also – may the British forgive him! – the bizarre one on 'Rule, Britannia'.) There are works such as Bach's Goldberg Variations, whose pensive aria is followed by a succession of diverse character pictures; on the other hand, in Mozart's Duport Variations, Beethoven's Diabelli Variations or Liszt's Variations on 'Weinen, Klagen, Sorgen, Zagen' the character of the theme remains decisive. In the Diabelli Variations there is room for a number of sublime and depressive pieces; yet, psychologically, the theme determines the course of the entire work.

It is not difficult to discover those variations that laugh or leap. (To spot the laughing, giggling or cackling, just apply the syllables ha-ha, hey-hey, hee-hee to the music and see whether they fit.) But there are also variations of a latent humour: they display, as in 1 and 9, characters deeply serious but slightly lacking in brains, or, as in 23, 27 and 28, one-track minds in an excited state. In the context of this work, they should be taken, and delivered, with more than a grain of irony.

I have devised a series of titles for the Diabelli Variations to amuse myself, but also for practical purposes. In a cycle of variations or other shorter pieces, the switch from one character to the next has to be prompt and secure, the characters themselves sharply defined, and clearly set apart from one another. In a song cycle or Liszt's *Années de pèlerinage*, the performer is guided by poems, and other literary allusions. Where they are missing, or composers are unwilling to operate with extra-musical images, the performer may find it useful to develop an acute verbal awareness of contrast, character and atmosphere to aid his psychological memory. Chopin's Preludes – pieces by a composer who always steered clear of poetic 'associations' – have inspired pianists such as Anton Rubinstein and Alfred Cortot to

invent titles which undoubtedly helped them to sustain a
great performance. Uhde, in a stimulating list,[1] has defined
the Diabelli Variations in the manner of Bartók's *Mikrokos-*
*mos*, a different approach that tries to encompass the variety
of characters mainly in musical terms. In his titles, descrip-
tions like 'Invention', 'Imitation', 'Accents' or 'Relaxed
Upbeats' remain on strictly musical ground, while images like
'Columns', 'Cascades', 'Loop', 'Crystal' or 'Swirl' are used
more rarely. In addition to the titles, Uhde specifies the
sound of each variation as being that of a string quartet, an
orchestra, an organ, a wind ensemble, a mixture of groups,
or the piano itself.

I could also imagine a view of the variations that employs
the four classical elements – earth, air, fire and water – as
tools for differentiation. Variations 1 and 9 are clearly
terrestrial, Var. 20 is subterranean. Fire blazes in Vars. 16/17
and 23. The gentle flow of water informs Vars. 12 and 26,
while Vars. 2 and 33 suspend gravity, and float in the air. In
some of the variations, elements appear combined (the
impossible becomes true, if only in music): in Vars. 6 and 27
there is a fusion of fire and water, in Var. 13 of earth and air.
Var. 10 shows simultaneously characteristics of air, fire and
water; and the fugue, which starts as an amalgam of earth
and fire, turns into water at the entrance of its third subject.

While these verbal crutches share the feature that they are
contrived in all seriousness, Wilhelm von Lenz's titles of 1860
– the first ever to be printed – bear witness to this Tsarist
privy councillor's quirky mind and sense of humour. Var. 1 is
called 'The Mastodon and the Theme – a fable'; Var. 7
occurs 'In the Tyrol'; and the facetious word 'Raptus'
(tantrum) is applied to Vars. 6, 23, 26 and 27. My own titles,
written down before I encountered those by Lenz, try in
similar spirit to illuminate Beethoven's 'rosy mood' or,
rather, to hint at his own degree of seriousness and
amusement.

---

[1] pp. 554–5

| | |
|---|---|
| Theme: | Alleged waltz |
| Var. 1: | March: gladiator, flexing his muscles |
| 2: | Snowflakes |
| 3: | Confidence and nagging doubt |
| 4: | Learned ländler |
| 5: | Tamed goblin |
| 6: | Trill rhetorics (Demosthenes braving the surf) |
| 7: | Swivelling and stamping |
| 8: | Intermezzo (to Brahms) |
| 9: | Industrious nutcracker |
| 10: | Giggling and neighing |
| 11: | 'Innocente' (Bülow) |
| 12: | Wave pattern |
| 13: | Aphorism, biting |
| 14: | Here He Cometh, the Chosen |
| 15: | Cheerful spook |
| 16/17: | Triumph |
| 18: | Precious memory, slightly faded |
| 19: | Helter-skelter |
| 20: | Inner sanctum |
| 21: | Maniac and moaner |
| 22: | 'Notte e giorno faticar' (to Diabelli) |
| 23: | The virtuoso at boiling-point (to Cramer) |
| 24: | Pure spirit |
| 25: | 'Teutscher' (German dance) |
| 26: | Circles on the water |
| 27: | Juggler |
| 28: | The rage of the jumping-jack |
| 29: | 'Stifled sighs' (Konrad Wolff) |
| 30: | Gentle grief |
| 31: | To Bach (to Chopin) |
| 32: | To Handel |
| 33: | To Mozart; to Beethoven |

'To Beethoven'? In the coda of the concluding variation, Beethoven speaks on his own behalf. He alludes to another supreme set of variations, that from his own last Sonata, Op. 111, which had been composed before the Diabelli Varia-

tions were finished. Beethoven's Arietta from Op. 111 is not
only in the same key as Diabelli's 'waltz', but also shares
certain motivic and structural features, while the characters
of the two themes could not be more disparate. One can hear
the Arietta as yet another, more distant, offspring of the
'waltz', and marvel at the inspirational effect of the 'cobbler's
patch'.

# VII

How do the ten variations of 1823 fit into the corpus of
pieces composed four years earlier? What do they add? Vars.
1 and 2 give a broader base to the 'group of ascent' which, if
we follow Uhde, incorporates the first ten variations in a
gradual increase of speed or density, a group that contains
Var. 8 as a well-nigh Brahmsian 'intermezzo'. Vars. 15 and
25 are inserted to remind us, as 'parodies' (Kinderman), of
the initial theme. Vars. 23–26 extend what Uhde calls the
'scherzo group' (Vars. 21–28), introducing into it the
contrast of the Fughetta (Var. 24) as a sublime sort of 'trio'
(Uhde). At the end of this group, Var. 28 provides the final
climax of agitation before we are plunged from extroversion
into inner darkness. Here, with the addition of Vars. 29 and
31, the single C minor variation of 1819 (30) now becomes
part of a larger C minor area. The expanding grief and
desolation of these pieces corresponds to their remoteness
from the theme's structure. But these elegies also fulfil
another, large-scale need. A great set of variations, Tovey
tells us, has 'the enormous momentum of something that
revolves on its axis or moves in an orbit. The highest problem
in the art of variation-making is to stop this momentum.'[1] In
the Diabelli Variations, the slow *minore* variations act as a
brake to which the reinvigorating fugue responds, not as a
finale (being in E flat major) but as an elemental experience,

---

[1] *Beethoven*, p. 125

a purifying ordeal from which the 'waltz' emerges transformed, 'reborn'. Do I detect a touch of Orphean mysteries
and Masonic initiation rites? I shall, rather, turn to Heinrich
von Kleist's wonderful essay 'On the Marionette Theatre'.
Near the end, there is a sentence that reads like an outline of
the Diabelli Variations: 'When perception has passed
through infinity, gracefulness reappears.' I wonder whether
Beethoven knew it.

*(1989)*

# The Text and its Guardians

## *Notes on Beethoven's Piano Concertos*

If musical errors drag on, those performers responsible can be said to fall into three groups. The first, enthralled by printer's ink, read music as uncritically as most people read their newspaper: they simply believe what they see. For the second type, the composer is an object of loathing. What they want is not a father-figure but some kind of musical parthenogenesis. Did the composer actually exist? And assuming he did, what does it matter today? Did he really know what he was doing? At any rate, we know better.

Somewhere in the middle are those musicians who do not take the trouble to ascertain that their text is correct. For them, life is too short for the fine print. They are happy to play the large print, whatever that may be, and with no matter what distortions it has arrived on the page.

Because of musicians like these, some fundamental misunderstandings in Beethoven's piano concertos linger on. Another reason is that a modern *Urtext* edition of these works has long been overdue. Bärenreiter has now remedied the situation at least for the concertos Opp. 15, 19 and 37; the editor is Hans-Werner Küthen.

The delay in the availability of a new edition has been connected with the strange fate of the autograph of Beethoven's C minor Concerto. After 1945 it was considered lost. But many years later it turned up in a Polish library, and was finally handed back to the Deutsche Staatsbibliothek in East Berlin. In the autograph the metre of the first movement is **C**, not the habitual *alla breve*. This, of course, will not come as a surprise to anybody who has consulted Franz Kullak's edition for two pianos (1881) or Carl Czerny's essay 'On the Correct Performance of all Beethoven's Piano

Works' in his Pianoforte School Op. 500 (1842). Unfortunately, the *alla breve* marking appears in the old Breitkopf & Härtel complete edition (1862), and their scores and orchestral parts of the Beethoven concertos are still in general use. Since then, most editions have adopted it. In the Eulenburg pocket score it is just one of many contestable features, but the Kinsky-Halm Beethoven catalogue has it too, and so does the cadenza volume of the new complete edition by Henle. All original sources read 𝄴 .

Why so much fuss about a vertical stroke? Is it not more important to have 'the proper feeling' for a piece? Certainly, but the performer – for all the liberties he is entitled to claim – must be able to answer to the composer for that 'feeling'.

The difference between 𝄴 and 𝄵 can, on occasion, be great enough to move mountains. It has an influence not only on the beat (the placement of stresses within the bar) and the character but definitely also on the tempo; Beethoven demonstrated in his original metronome markings elsewhere – whether or not we wish to take them literally – that two tempo categories are indeed intended. We need hear no more than the first few bars of the C minor Concerto to realize what damage is done by an *alla breve*; the quavers of the opening theme lose their rhythmic footing. A chair that needs four legs is made to stand on two.

The men responsible for this misdeed are those in charge of the old complete edition: Gustav Nottebohm and Carl Reinecke. The second movement of the Fifth Concerto did not escape their blue pencil either; here, the authentic 𝄵 was altered to 𝄴 . (This was the more frequent procedure. In the old Mozart complete edition several concerto movements are 'corrected' in such a manner.)

Playing the Adagio un poco mosso of the Fifth Concerto as solemnly as possible has become an impressive habit. Again, Czerny and Kullak are the only ones to give the correct metre, *alla breve*; Czerny does so quite specifically with the words 'the Adagio (alla breve) should not drag' (*darf nicht schleppend gehn*). It was Czerny, after all, who gave the first Vienna performance in 1812 under Beethoven's eyes.

Czerny's comments on Beethoven's piano works are available, in German and English, in an annotated edition by Paul Badura-Skoda (Universal Edition). They remain the most important source of information that has come down to us about the performance of these works. Czerny's metronome figures for the first movements of the Concertos Opp. 15, 19 and 37 strike me as a convincing product of practical experience; they can at least be taken as approximate values. Although the three movements have the same tempo marking, *allegro con brio*, they are given metronome figures corresponding to the individual character: Op. 15, ♩ = 88, or more correctly ♩ = 176; Op. 19, ♩ = 152; Op. 37 ♩ = 144. With brisk activity and an alert intentness in common, they do have different things to say. The driving tempo of the C major Concerto counteracts any feeling of *maestoso*; it makes sense if the pianist is not afraid to see the development as a piece within a piece – a more restrained, and romantic, sphere from which the listener is suddenly propelled by the fortissimo octave run before the recapitulation. I do not recall any other Beethoven Allegro in which the development has been placed so noticeably in parenthesis.

In the slow movements, however, Czerny's sometimes rather hurried speeds remind me of the late Hans Schmidt-Isserstedt's pun: 'Spielen Sie flüssig, aber nicht überflüssig' ('Be fluent but not superfluous').

Three more textual corrections should be mentioned:

1.  In the Adagio of the B flat Concerto the demisemiquaver in bars 76 and 79 must be read as a semiquaver.
2.  In the first movement of the C minor Concerto there are three 'new' bars in the timpani part (334–336).
3.  In the cadenza of the C minor Concerto the bass octave $G_1$-G, two bars before the double trill, is missing in both complete editions although it looms large in the autograph. (A facsimile edition of Beethoven's cadenzas was published by Eulenburg in 1979.)

In the G major Concerto, I make use of a few alterations and corrections by Beethoven himself, published by Paul

Badura-Skoda in *Österreichische Musikzeitschrift*, October 1958. I also recommend looking through the solo part of the Fifth Concerto in Clementi's London edition which, as we have learnt from Alan Tyson, was published simultaneously with the Leipzig first print. May I assure all doubting Thomases that the cadenza I play in the first movement of the Fourth Concerto is indeed Beethoven's own; the autograph has the superscription *Cadenza ma senza cadere*, an allusion to its pianistic pitfalls. I have often been asked why I should waste my time on this bizarre piece when another more lyrical, and plausible, cadenza is available. I think that the Cadenza ma senza cadere adds something to our knowledge of Beethoven. It shows almost shockingly how Beethoven the architect could turn, in some of his cadenzas, into a genius running amok. Almost all the classical principles of order fall by the wayside, as comparison with Mozart's cadenzas will amply demonstrate. Breaking away from the style and character of the movement does not bother Beethoven at all, and harmonic detours cannot be daring enough. No other composer has ever offered cadenzas of such provoking madness.

The warning 'ma senza cadere' reminds me of another tendency of Beethoven the virtuoso – that of stretching the player's bravura to new limits. In a few cases these limits are, either mischievously or erroneously, overstretched. The brilliant broken octave triplets in the first movement of the Sonata Op. 2 No. 2 (bars 84 ff.) are provided with a fingering that flies in the face of reason: it is in any tempo impracticable, and in the prescribed *allegro moderato* unplayable. (Even such a literal-minded Beethovenian as Heinrich Schenker recommended the use of both hands.)

Another case that amounts almost to a practical joke is his four-hand setting of the 'Grosse Fuge', in which he simply keeps the violins for the primo player, and leaves the viola and cello for the secondo, regardless of all crossings between the voices.

Then there is the octave passage immediately before the recapitulation in the first movement of the C major Concer-

to. What Beethoven wrote down is doubly confusing: there
are fortissimo semiquaver octaves in the right hand, but also
a bass note G in the left. This note is marked *forte*, whereas
the strings coming in at the same downbeat have *pianissimo*.
The editor of the Henle score suggests in his critical comments that, in order not to lose the bass note, 'fast legato
octaves' should be played by the right hand. I have heard a
performance (and pitied its conductor) where the soloist had
decided on a kind of snail's pace for the whole movement in
order to give those octaves their due. If this is faithful to the
maxim that every note has to be played in the way the
composer wrote it down – a maxim I would not accept
without reservations – it is quite damaging to the exhilarating
spirit of this piece. Furthermore, fast octaves were evidently
not part of Beethoven's technical equipment; unlike Weber
or Schubert, he never used them at all – unless they are
glissando octaves indicated by slurs. Our octave run is
slurred, and so are the runs in the stretta of the 'Waldstein'
Sonata. Czerny refers to both as glissando passages.

What does the musical situation demand? The dreamy
atmosphere of the organ point, sustained by the horns, and
surrounded by diminished-seventh chords in a haze of pedal,
is brusquely terminated. With the entry of the first fortissimo
octave, two bars before the actual recapitulation, the initial
character returns: brisk, witty and wide-awake. The pianissimo in the strings seems to indicate that Beethoven intended a
fortissimo to appear only two bars later. When (subsequently?) writing down the solo part, Beethoven may have
forgotten to adjust the dynamics.[1] If this adjustment is made,
and the strings played forte, the pianist's bass note becomes
redundant. But there is an even better solution, albeit a less
literal one: Edwin Fischer started the passage an octave
higher and played, from there, a double glissando, beginning after the bass note. While this surpasses the compass of
Beethoven's instrument, and ignores the printed semiquaver

---

[1] Unfortunately, the autograph does not bear out this assumption; the octave run
was evidently written first.

rhythm, it seems to suit the psychological idea to perfection, and blends admirably with the pre-Lisztian piano style of the (later) grand cadenza. It might well have amused Beethoven to know that there have been pianists who, perplexed by the notation of these bars, decided to stay away from the concerto altogether. Perhaps it would have pleased him to have dumbfounded performers whose trust in the composer's infallibility lacked the counterbalance of imagination, and critical scrutiny.

*(1983)*

# Beethoven's New Style

Beethoven's late style still strikes me as unexpected and prodigious. Everything by way of preparation, all the various portents and new departures apparent in works like the Opp. 74 and 95 Quartets or the Sonatas 'quasi una fantasia' Op. 27 hardly mitigate the astonishing impression made by the two great Cello Sonatas Op. 102. They still come as a violent shock, as they did to Beethoven's contemporaries – the beginning of a new style so diverse as to elude definition.

Until 1812, Beethoven's output had continued without interruption; the B flat Piano Trio Op. 97, the Seventh and Eighth Symphonies (Opp. 92 and 93) and the Op. 96 Violin Sonata had brilliantly signalled the end of an era in instrumental music, during which the transition from early to middle-period Beethoven – in so far as such simplifications are acceptable at all – had proceeded smoothly and, as it were, of its own accord. The years 1813–14 mark a pause. Besides the revision of *Fidelio*, they are taken up with those unworthy showpieces *Wellington's Victory* and *Der glorreiche Augenblick*, which represent the summit of Beethoven's public fame. The only instrumental work belonging to these years, apart from the Polonaise Op. 89, is the intimate Op. 90 Piano Sonata, at once a throwback and a forerunner. The following year, after his brother's death from consumption, Beethoven plunged with tragic zeal into a new role as his nephew's guardian. The pain associated with this relationship remained with him to the end of his life. Illness and real or imaginary money troubles helped to increase the effort required to complete a work. The cello sonatas of 1815 in particular seem to have been a threshold painful to cross. In 1816 the final rupture of relations between Beethoven and Therese Brunswick's sister Josephine (von Stakelberg, formerly Countess Deym) contributed towards making this a singularly trying time in Beethoven's life. Yet the influence of biographical events on Beethoven's manner of composition should not be exaggerated; the slowing down in his working procedures may well be explained by the greater density and complexity of his later style. Works like the Sonata Op. 106, the Diabelli Variations, the *Missa solemnis* or the Ninth Symphony needed extended planning and preparation. They concentrate Beethoven's entire composing experience into huge, bold syntheses while, at the same time, requiring new means of expression to be developed and tested.

Synthesis and expansion of resources – that is where a description of Beethoven's late style would have to begin. Direct opposites are forced together. A new intricacy is matched by its antithesis, a new naïvety. Apparent exaggeration is juxtaposed with apparent artlessness, abruptness with a novel, relaxed lyricism. Simple, primitive, popular and vulgar elements all find their place in the music without damaging its structure. Martin Cooper has pointed out the use of two popular songs, 'Unsa Kätz häd Katzln ghabt' ('Our cat has had kittens') and 'Ich bin lüderlich, du bist lüderlich' ('I am draggletailed, you are draggletailed'), in the second movement of Op. 110.

The complexity of Beethoven's late style may be broken down into a new delicacy and density of detail, and a new rigour and refinement of its polyphonic part-writing. Diversity of detail now complements the spacious grandeur of the 'Waldstein' and 'Appassionata' Sonatas, the 'Emperor' Concerto, or the 'Archduke' Trio. But there is also a new attitude towards the miniature: as with the slow introduction to the finale of Op. 101 or the scherzo of Op. 106, extremely concise forms are incorporated within the context of large ones, though they may also be left on their own, as in the late Bagatelles. (Incidentally, it was precisely these pieces which were grossly misunderstood by some of Beethoven's contemporaries, as shown by Schindler's contemptuous remarks about the Op. 126 set.)

The new polyphony which, even in the most homophonic sections, now pervades Beethoven's part-writing is a first indication that, in his late works, baroque influences are more evident than ever before. This polyphony 'turns the bass into melody' (Walter Riezler) and provides in some of his late sonatas, his B flat Quartet, the Diabelli Variations, the *Missa solemnis*, and the finale of the Ninth, climaxes with the aid of fugal form. Other baroque features that have left their mark are the recitative, the (sometimes richly ornamented) aria, and the chaconne. As for Beethoven's new polyphony, it makes his music not only more refined, but also a great deal more radical and uncompromising. Even Hans von Bülow, who used to play all the last five sonatas in one evening and possibly did more than anyone else to popularize them, found it necessary to 'dilute' a few instances of the 'Hammerklavier' fugue. It took Schoenberg and Bartók to carry on where Beethoven's late polyphony had left off.

One of Beethoven's uncompromising traits is his predilection for clashing seconds (as when the basic note and the suspension are sounded together). This had already been apparent in the 'Lebewohl' Sonata Op. 81a, where the telescoping of the horn-calls which so graphically depicts the disappearance of the coach aroused misgivings well into the nineteenth century. Nor is Beethoven afraid of writing false relations. Another feature is the wide separation of the registers, of treble and bass. Finicky listeners have blamed Beethoven's deafness for all this. If it was indeed his deafness that brought out the use of such artistic means, we should be grateful for it.

With this exploitation of extreme registers goes a new 'geographical' awareness of sound – not of spatial depth, as in the 'Waldstein' Sonata, but of 'deep down' and 'high above', or indeed of 'subterranean' and 'stratospheric'. Here, the fourth variation from Op. 111 provides a magical example.

Apart from clashing seconds, false relations and suspensions, the characteristics of Beethoven's late style include syncopations, bold leaping intervals and chromatic transitional harmonies. Perfect cadences are, wherever possible, avoided or 'veiled' (Riezler), while church modes mysteriously expand tonality. Like the 'open endings' of the last three sonatas, they are among those attributes of Beethoven's late music that have aroused religious associations. Did Beethoven, in his late works, progress from the personal to the universal? His *Missa solemnis*, and the grand invocations to the 'Creator' and 'Dear Father' in the Ninth have certainly provided powerful arguments to support this assumption. The roughly opposing view, however, has also found its adherents; resting on the observation that Beethoven showed less regard than ever for the 'wretched fiddles', the wretched throats or wretched ears of his contemporaries – that is to say, the accepted usages of listening and playing – it suggests that Beethoven retreated from the universally accessible into subjectivity. Simplifications of this kind cannot possibly do justice to the richness of a style that embraces past, present and future, the sublime and the profane.

## Sonata Op. 101

Dorothea Ertmann's incomparable performance of the rondo from Op. 90 was praised by Schindler. In dedicating the A major Sonata Op. 101 to the Baroness, Beethoven was doing more than merely repaying a debt of courtesy. Having been a pupil of Beethoven's for many years, she became a personal friend and one of the best interpreters of his piano music. (And how much Op. 101 in particular needs a confident and initiated player!) To some, she even seemed to qualify as a candidate for Beethoven's 'Immortal Beloved', a notion dispelled by recent scholarship. It is interesting, however, that another masterpiece of 1816, the song cycle *An die ferne Geliebte*, shares with Op. 101 the characteristic of recalling its opening theme at a later stage.

In the sonata, the tenderly questioning phrase that opened the first movement reappears between the Adagio and the finale with a visionary quality. This kind of harking back to earlier movements, as also practised in the Cello Sonata Op. 102 No. 1 and the finale of the Ninth, was later beloved of

the Romantics. Altogether, this sonata had great impact on
Romantic composers; the second movement affected Schumann's style more than anything else by Beethoven, and the
cantabile lyricism of the first not only left clear traces in
Mendelssohn's Sonata Op. 6 but also caused Mendelssohn's
musical opponent Wagner to remark that his own ideal of
'unending melody' had here already been realized.

Op. 101 marks a fundamental change in Beethoven's
sonatas. Formerly, the sum of the movements resulted in a
perfect balance. Now, the dynamic, developmental aspect of
his composing takes hold over the entire work; the last
movement becomes the climax to which everything leads: it
gathers together the forces which in the earlier movements
have been pulling in different directions, or surpasses the
first movement by the conviction of a superior, and opposite,
position, as in Op. 111. The rondo form, unsuitable for this
kind of intensification, is now abandoned. The scherzo, when
present at all, moves to second place before the slow
movement; so far has it shifted from the conventional
scherzo pattern that Beethoven from now on grants this title
only to the second movement of Op. 106. Even sonata forms
no longer appear without some element of strangeness: they
may do without contrast (Op. 101); or contain development
sections simpler than those of Mozart's most serene sequences (Op. 110); or they unite, as composite forms, with
scherzo and fugue. Final movements are now reserved for
strict counterpoint or for a set of slow variations. Although
the finale of Op. 101 is a sonata form, its imitative polyphony
is agglomerated, in the development section, into a fugue.

Op. 101 is not an exuberant work. In it, as Wagner
observed, passionate outbursts are out of the question. It
does not belong to the line of spiritual dramas that 'wrestle
with the elements' or 'quarrel with fate'. All the happiness, all
the power and assurance with which the sonata is imbued are
imparted with supreme composure. It does not overwhelm
and compel like Op. 106, nor does it release mysterious
sources of feeling with the immediacy of the last three
sonatas. The brief Adagio does not sing out its melancholy

like the ariosi of Op. 110 – played *una corda*, it communes
with itself in a whisper, reticent and clear-sighted. As may be
gathered from Beethoven's indications, the tempi avoid
extremes throughout: the Allegretto not too flowing, the
Adagio not too slow, the last movement 'fast, but not too
much so'; and the 'march-like' second movement, which was
marked 'ziemlich lebhaft' (lively enough) in the autograph,
lost its 'ziemlich' in the first print.[1]

## Sonata Op. 106

Even today, this work shows up the outer limits of what a
composer of sonatas can accomplish, a performer can
control, or a listener can take in. In a magnificent exertion of
will, it combines grandeur and delicacy, the grand sweep and
extreme density of detail. The player should muster endurance as well as boldness, fierce intensity as well as the cool
grasp of a panoramic overview.

Czerny, who had played the sonata for Beethoven,
describes the tempo of the first movement as 'uncommonly
fast and fiery'. The initial theme relates to the rhythm of the
words 'vivat, vivat, Rudolphus'; it was the Archduke Rudolph
to whom the sonata was dedicated. Two elements, the
tension between the keys of B flat major and B minor, and
the interval of the third, are decisive in the unfolding of the
vast design. The intrusion of B minor (the 'black key',
according to Beethoven) into the recapitulation of the first
movement has grave consequences: not until the final fugue
is this conflict resolved. In the coda of the scherzo, eerie
juxtapositions of B flat and B natural bare the problem to its
bones. We encounter the 'black key' once more at a
declamatory climax of the Adagio ('con grand' espressione')
and, finally, in the cancrizans of the fugue. For both B flat

---

[1] In this context 'ziemlich' does not suggest moderation. Beethoven himself, in *An
die ferne Geliebte*, translated 'ziemlich geschwind' as *assai allegro* (suitably/sufficiently
fast).

major and B minor, the related thirds are G and D; these are the only tones the two keys have in common. In G major, there is the second thematic group of the first movement, and the inversion of the fugue. The 'religious' D major sphere is given to secondary themes of the Adagio and the fugue.

Beethoven's special contribution as a fugal composer is the turbulent and frenzied fugue that nearly, but only nearly, defies the strictures of contrapuntal writing. Boundless energy and intellectual rigour have never been coupled at a higher pitch of excitement.

The slow introduction of the fugue resembles in its psychological situation the final movement of Beethoven's Op. 110: after its 'exhausted lament' vital forces gradually reappear. The Adagio itself, a 'mausoleum of collective suffering' (Lenz), is the depressive counterpart to the manic agitation of the fast movements. Its alternating sections of *una corda* and *tre corde* turn out to be different regions of sound and grief. (On Beethoven's pianos, the quality of sound produced by the soft pedal was more shadowy and fragile than it is today, a sphere of whispering and subdued *mezza voce* singing.) To join the end of the Adagio and the beginning of the Largo in performance seems to me a psychological mistake; listeners and players ought to have the chance to draw breath.

Two contentious issues challenge the performer to a decision. The first relates to whether A natural or A sharp should be played before the start of the recapitulation. I have never doubted that A natural is what Beethoven wanted. It seems obvious that Beethoven, on the evidence of the harmonic progression, forgot to put in the natural sign. In Tovey[1] we find a very good collection of arguments for the natural, the most important being Beethoven's own harmonic sketch for this passage and the downright orthographical improbability of A sharp and F in the same bar. Furth-

---

[1] *A Companion to Beethoven's Pianoforte Sonatas*, p. 218

ermore, Paul Badura-Skoda[1] has shown that, on this particular page of the first edition, a host of mistakes and omissions
has remained uncorrected. A psychological point should be
added: anyone who rejects the reasonable and expected in
favour of the 'audacity of genius' embodied in the A sharp
should consider whether, at this moment of the piece, such a
surprise move in the bass serves any useful purpose. Should
not the resounding entry of the recapitulation lull us into a
sense of security? Should we not think we have returned
home before the modulation via G flat major to B minor
destroys our illusion? This can only be imparted by a bass
progression that does not skip the leading-note A, and with it
the whole cadence.

The second bone of contention concerns Beethoven's
metronome marks. I must confess that to me they do not,
even in conception, seem wholly appropriate to the character
of the movements, with the possible exception of the Largo
introduction to the fugue. The indication ($\downarrow$ = 138) for the
first movement is – by any player, and on any piano – simply
unworkable; not for nothing did Beethoven himself change
his mind about the original Allegro assai, deleting the *assai*.
Let us, by all means, play this movement 'fast and fiery', yet
leave enough room for its wide range of colour and dynamics
to emerge.

The first London printing, which appeared almost simultaneously with the Viennese edition by Artaria, offers by
comparison several interesting corrections, additions and
alternatives. It may be mentioned as a curiosity that in the
English edition the Adagio comes before the scherzo. In a
letter to his pupil Ferdinand Ries in London, Beethoven
himself allowed the option of interchanging the inner
movements at will or even omitting the Largo before the
fugue, suggestions that seem to defy sanity.

---

[1] *Musik, Edition, Interpretation*, Gedenkschrift für Günter Henle (1980), pp. 58–9

## Sonatas Opp. 109, 110 and 111

The last trilogy of sonatas (1820–22) was written in conjunction with Beethoven's work on the *Missa solemnis*. All three have in common a new way of ending. Where the last chords of Op. 106 had finished off the work in an unequivocal manner, Op. 109 withdraws into an inner world, Op. 110 ends in euphoric self-immolation, while Op. 111 surrenders itself to silence.

Two movements in sonata form precede the superb variations of the E major Sonata Op. 109. They are fundamentally different in character. The quasi-improvised, dreamlike first movement suspends gravity; the second is an excitable outburst veering between anger and fear. In the first movement the bass hovers in syncopation behind the notes of the melody, hardly touching the ground. In the second it makes itself all the more clearly felt: clinging to the ground, yet unable to impose stability as it remains almost entirely rooted in the dominant. The first movement glides along in a single rhythmic pattern, interrupted by the declamatory second theme in a new tempo and time-signature; it has light colours, long breath-spans and un-dulating contours. On the other hand, the second movement is dark, flickering and jagged, jerky and short-winded; within the 6/8 time the rhythm is diverse; the subsidiary ideas offer no contrast, but in the main theme itself there is competition between the melody and the bass, which dominates the development section on its own.

The final movement combines the essence of the first with the aspirations of the second; it both floats along and brings repose. Czerny wanted it played 'in the style of Handel and Seb. Bach'. Indeed, Handel's influence reveals itself at once in the sarabande-like variation theme – if we disregard Beethoven's extremely sensitive dynamic indications.

In 1821 Beethoven wrote: 'From last year until now I have been ill all the time, over the summer I also caught jaundice ... now, thank God, it is going better and good health finally seems to want to put new life into me ...' The experience of abating and returning powers had left its mark on works both earlier and later than the A flat Sonata Op. 110. Already the 'Hammerklavier' Sonata had gathered up new musical energy in the introduction to its fugue, and in the 'Heiliger Dankgesang' from the Op. 132 Quartet we read 'Feeling new strength'.

As with the Opp. 101, 109 and 111 Sonatas, the thematic fundamentals of Op. 110 are the space of six adjacent diatonic notes (a hexachord) and the intervals of a third and a fourth which subdivide it. Whether the motifs rise or fall within the sixth remains important throughout the piece. In the caressing cantabile of the first movement it is not the slender development section but the subsidiary theme that imparts a notion of excitement; here contrary motion combines ascending and descending lines. The apparently static development section shows the opening theme in a crisis – unable to rise to the sixth, its first two bars wander around in regions of minor tonality. The restoration of the theme in the recapitulation then gives the impression of breathing freely again; here, its left-hand answering phrase even manages to overreach the hexachord.

The second movement, a piece in the style of the late Bagatelles, is dominated entirely by contrary motion. D'Albert tried to read into it a gavotte with accents on every second bar, yet the capricious character of the piece and the justification for the 2/4 notation both stem precisely from its frequent changes of accentuation, and from the fact that the bar pattern before the trio and coda becomes confused in a manner half burlesque and half mysteriously modal. The obdurate right-hand figuration in the trio may be construed as a sequence of thirds and fourths within the smallest possible space.

The third movement is Passion music – a complex of baroque forms in which ariosi and fugues are interwoven. The sections are arranged as follows: (1) *Recitative* (modulating from the F major close of the scherzo to A flat); (2) *Arioso dolente* (A flat minor); (3) *Fugue* (this part of the fugue remains an exposition; it does not leave the key of A flat major); (4) *Return of the Arioso in G minor* ('wearily lament-ing'); (5) *Inversion of the Fugue* ('gradually reviving' – a new start, but also a continuation of the first fugue as its modulating section, in which entries follow in close succes-sion); (6) *Homophonic conclusion in A flat major.*

In a movement for which Beethoven has left us such specific and meaningful instructions as 'wearily lamenting', one may assume a large psychological context. What is the relationship of ariosi and fugues? The first part of the fugue attempts to counteract the 'lamenting song' – which, it has been noted, bears a resemblance to the aria 'It is finished' from Bach's St John Passion. There is no immediate healing effect; the second arioso shows this not only by its abrupt semitone drop but also by the way in which the melodic line becomes porous, expressing, with its continual sighs and pauses for breath, the reduced resistance of the sufferer. (In the Cavatina of the Op. 130 Quartet the singing line in the 'beklemmt' (stifled, constricted) return of the arioso is similarly fragmented.)

Ten gently swelling, syncopated G major chords emerge from the closing bar 'like a reawakening heartbeat' (Edwin Fischer). The inverted fugue theme then appears, as unreal as a mirage. The ensuing process reluctantly leads back to reality. Its path is not made easy for the listener – and it obviously did not come easily to Beethoven. Stretti, progres-sive diminution of the theme, and tempo changes all obey the law of continual foreshortening; they are musical symbols of returning vitality, but also stages in a dissolution of fugal constraints. Polyphony becomes a burden to be shaken off. The opening theme, augmented and syncopated, vainly resists the collapse of polyphony. Its augmentation is gradually reduced to the initial outline of the theme, which enters in the bass when the return to A flat major is accomplished. At last, the dominance of fugal polyphony is broken, the goal of revival attained. The remainder of the movement is a lyrical hymn. In a last euphoric effort, its conclusion reaches out beyond homophonic emancipation, throwing off the chains of music itself.

Beethoven's C minor Sonata Op. 111 leaves a dual impression – it is the final testimony of his sonatas as well as a prelude to silence. Its two movements confront each other as thesis and antithesis. We recall attempts at interpretation, such as 'Samsara and Nirvana' (Bülow), the 'Worldly and Otherworldly' (Fischer), 'Resistance and Submission' (Lenz), or the masculine and feminine principles which Beethoven himself was so fond of expounding.

In the context of musical form this contrast is one of animation against repose. The forms with the most compelling animation are sonata and fugue; the Allegro of Op. 111 is a sonata form suffused with fugal elements. The form representing tranquil constancy within change is a set of variations; the Adagio of Op. 111 is again a variation movement, its progressive rhythmic foreshortening even more consistently realized than in the finale of Op. 109.

Once more, the beginning of the first movement immediately determines its basic character, one of angry revolt. At the same time it provides a thematic seed for the whole sonata: E flat – C – B natural in downward motion. Psychologically and materially, Schubert's setting of Heine's 'Der Atlas' is closely akin to it. The *maestoso* introduction and the main Allegro relate to one another as dominant and tonic. With his tempo marking *Allegro con brio ed appassionato*, Beethoven makes clear that he is not enthroned on Olympus. In the Adagio the words *semplice e cantabile* aim to show performers the way. What they imply is not ingenuousness or simple-minded sweetness, but simplicity as a result of complexity – distilled experience.

*(1976)*

# Schubert's Last Sonatas

## I

Schubert's death deprived us of a wealth of possible masterpieces, though hardly, as Franz Grillparzer's epitaph suggests, of even fairer accomplishment. The last three sonatas should not be taken as a final message. As far as we know, they were composed in the brief period between May and September 1828. The fair copy was made just a few weeks before Schubert died of typhoid, his constitution already weakened by syphilis and by a burst of productivity frantic even by his standards. Since the death of his mother, he may have had to come to terms with a growing awareness of his own mortality. Yet, when he completed his last sonatas (and most probably also the C major Quintet) in the autumn of 1828, it seems to me that he had no intimation of imminent death.

The style of Schubert's last year is not in any sense the kind of late style which I can perceive (*pace* Wolfgang Hildesheimer) in late Mozart. Admittedly, in the first two movements of Schubert's B flat Sonata, in the Adagio of the C minor Sonata and in the slow movement of the String Quintet, a new gentle, serene, hymnic facet can be identified; but this is less surprising if we consider the Mass in E flat, a major achievement of the same period, which left its mark on the instrumental music composed during those hectic months, just as it in turn was marked by the expressionism of the Heine songs. Plagal harmonies, like those which conclude the Gloria and 'Et incarnatus' of the Mass, can be found not only at the close of some sonata movements but also at the heart of the A major Sonata's first subject which, in the first draft, was conceived without the energetic left-hand leaps, in the manner of a chorale:

Many other themes in Schubert's sonata trilogy are based on or contain plagal harmonies as well.

The opening of the B flat Sonata also belongs in this 'sacred' sphere. Schubert offers solemn introspection, while Mozart's Piano Concerto K.595 in the same key seems to suggest, in its deceptive simplicity, childhood regained. There is, however, common ground: in the vocal character of the melodies, in the undemonstrative calm with which both works unfold and in their all-pervading melancholy.

The reappearance of a B flat major theme in the remote musical perspective of B minor, at the beginning of the development in K.595, reminds us of Schubert's passion for chromatic neighbouring keys. In his B flat Sonata, Schubert himself brings off an unforgettable harmonic projection of a very different kind: at the end of the development he quotes, *pianississimo*, his main theme in the tonic key of B flat – yet we experience it, in relation to the surrounding D minor sphere, as if from the remotest distance. When, only a few lines later on, the theme is restated in its original guise, our standpoint has changed completely; by now the theme, in its gentle serenity, has come so close that the listener can sense it as if from within.

# II

Our perception of this theme is crucial for understanding the whole movement. Its trill (bar 8) has been described as a 'disturbing foreign element' (Dieter Schnebel)[1] or as a

---

[1] Dieter Schnebel, 'Schubert: Auf der Suche nach der befreiten Zeit', *Denkbare Musik*, 1972

'*Movens*' in contrast to the '*Quietiv*' of the calmly soaring melody (August Halm)[1]. I prefer to see it as the disclosure of a third dimension.

The pause allows the sound to disappear as if into infinity. There is no break in continuity – the dominant chord easily carries the tension through the pause to the next tonic; rather, a rapport is established between music and silence. (The timpani roll in the Sanctus of the Mass in E flat is a comparable case.) Schubert's first draft, which consists almost entirely of the melody, already contains this trill; but it also contains the notes G–F in the fourth bar, to which the trill relates.

[1] August Halm, *Beethoven*, 1927

The G flat trill could be called a darkened reflection of these notes. The major and minor second and their combination G – G flat – F continue to remain prominent. In the bass, F and G flat determine much of the exposition. A variant of the first subject reappears almost immediately (bar 20) in G flat: it seems as if, over a distance of eleven bars, the first trill has caused the second one to descend. Later a new, pleading theme is introduced in F sharp minor, and the development begins a fifth higher, in C sharp minor, which is also the key of the second movement. C sharp and F sharp are again present, as D flat and G flat, in the scherzo.

Time after time the final movement recalls its opening G octave, forcefully emphasized in the manner of a *fp* horn accent. Here G flat is present only as a passing note between G and F; if this descent signifies a sigh, then it suggests comic relief rather than suffering or fatigue. In the touching epilogue, which seems to suspend time before the final stretta, the three-note descent emerges as a serious question. The ensuing bars subtly make us aware that G flat has ceased to pose a problem, and the sonata's '*Dolens*' (as I would call it) is finally overcome.

A brief presto coda exults in this achievement. Altogether, I find this movement distinguished by playful, graceful energy rather than by 'sighing fatigue' (Schnebel). Here, as in certain other points, Beethoven's last work, the B flat Rondo, written as an afterthought for his Op. 130 Quartet to replace the 'Grosse Fuge', offers a parallel.

# III

Artur Schnabel and Eduard Erdmann were, to my knowledge, the first to play Schubert's sonata trilogy in one evening. After one of my performances of this wonderful, if strenuous, programme, a Viennese newspaper pronounced that even if I, who had turned my back on Vienna, were to deny the fact, I must have 'experienced' these works while resident in Schubert's city. How these sonatas, *Die Winterreise* and the Heine songs, the Mass in E flat or the String Quintet could be 'experienced' in present-day Vienna was not disclosed. Not that Schubert had ever been the kind of provincial musician that a cosmopolitan like Busoni chose to see in him. His music shows no shortage of elements from far beyond the city gates: in the finale of the B flat Sonata we detect, perhaps, a Hungarian flavour; in the third of his Posthumous Piano Pieces D.946 there are Bohemian dance rhythms (polka and sousedská); and the macabre finale of the C minor Sonata turns out to be a tarantella, which, like the whole work, is spiritually much closer to the black fantasies of Goya than to Schubert's painter friends Kupelwieser and Schwind. Goya, incidentally, also died in 1828.

What is a 'Viennese composer'? (Besides Schubert, the critic mentioned Gustav Mahler and Alban Berg.) A composer — penalized for failing to imitate Johann Strauss — whose music was so disquieting that it had to be inflicted on the Viennese belatedly and with great effort? In a letter of 1827, Schubert describes Metternich's Vienna: 'It is certainly rather big, but makes up for this by an absence of warmth, of openness, true thought, sensible words and, in particular, of spirited deeds.' Even today, Vienna may be the right place for musicians to learn what a Strauss waltz is about. But it would be wishful thinking to claim that a Viennese Schubert tradition ever existed or still exists. Who in nineteenth-century Vienna, apart from Brahms and the Hellmesberger Quartet, took any interest in Schubert's instrumental music? (The Schubert enthusiasts Schumann, Mendelssohn, Liszt, Anton Rubinstein, Dvořák and George Grove were all occasional visitors.) How many of the great Schubert singers or conductors came from his home town or country? Where, until quite recently, were the Viennese pianists who championed Schubert's sonatas? For Sauer, Rosenthal and Godowsky they were of no consequence; they owe their discovery to Schnabel and Erdmann in the Berlin of the 1920s. True, Schnabel did study in Vienna, but, even if he had been advised to look at the unexplored Schubert sonatas, his teacher Leschetizky would scarcely have told him how they ought to be played.[1] Significantly, Schnabel's enormous influence as a teacher did not permeate Vienna at all.

Today, Vienna offers no more clues about Schubert than any other city. The panorama from the Belvedere may have remained unchanged since Schubert's time. But do people still live in one-room apartments — as Schubert's family did — and give birth to their children in an alcove which also serves as the kitchen? Do adults still play blind-man's-buff? Do manuscripts have to be submitted to the censor? Is the country governed by the secret police? Is that popular and suburban music which Schubert found so charming still a

---

[1] The Viennese element in the scherzo of Schubert's D major Sonata is grossly exaggerated in Schnabel's recording.

living musical presence, or just a beautiful relic of 'better days'? Even the Viennese assertion that 'Vienna remains Vienna' is no more than a Viennese delusion.

## IV

Schubert's last sonatas did not appear in print until eleven years after his death. Johann Nepomuk Hummel, a Mozart pupil and leading pianist, was Schubert's intended dedicatee; however, as Hummel died in 1837, the publishers decided on Schumann, who had warmly praised the E flat Piano Trio, the D minor Quartet and the piano sonatas in A minor (D.845), D major and G major in his *Neue Zeitschrift für Musik*. Regrettably, the last sonatas disappointed him. He criticized their 'much greater simplicity [*Einfalt*] of invention' and Schubert's 'spinning out of certain musical ideas, where usually between one period and the next he interweaves new threads'. If Schumann intended to imply a greater concentration of musical material and the use made of it – if, that is, we were to interpret *Einfalt* as 'unity' – we could agree and, unlike Schumann, approve. Alas, he also speaks of Schubert's 'voluntary renunciation of shining novelty, where he usually sets himself such high standards' and concludes: '[These pieces] ripple along from page to page as if without end, never in doubt as to how to continue, always musical and singable, interrupted here and there by stirrings of some vehemence which, however, are rapidly stilled.'

It is to be hoped that Schumann, in later years, became better acquainted with the works, and regretted his verdict. Not even from him will I accept that Schubert's sonatas 'ripple along'. The occasional 'stirrings of some vehemence' amount, not infrequently, to the grandest of dramatic developments if not, as in the C minor Sonata, the impetuosity of entire movements. As for a 'voluntary renunciation of novelty', the middle section of the A major Sonata's second movement alone should suffice as a striking refutation. Even today, this eruption of the irrational must rank among the most daring and terrifying pages in all music.


## V


'As if without end' – Schubert's 'length', which Schumann, writing two years later of the Great C major Symphony, considered 'heavenly', came to be deemed his principal weakness. When Mendelssohn conducted the C major Symphony in Leipzig, he felt obliged to make cuts; at the beginning of this century the pianist Harold Bauer produced an abridged version of the B flat Sonata. Growing familiarity with Brucknerian and Mahlerian dimensions has since relaxed our perception of musical space. Aesthetic appetites have changed. We experience marathon concerts, huge television serials, the six-hour *Hamlet* in Berlin – whispered and in slow motion – while neo-expressionist painters savage oversized canvases. Art is expected to forget all constraint, mix up disparate elements, be unreasonable, want more than it can achieve and achieve more than anybody can want. Boundless is beautiful. (The novel, on the other hand, which formerly encompassed entire worlds, has shrunk to something fragmentary, a dialogue between the writer and his obsessions.)

Schubert's music, which used to appear excessively long, is suddenly not long enough. Where some earlier pianists took the first movement of the B flat Sonata at an almost nervous *alla breve* (two beats to a bar), nowadays, in extreme cases, it is counted in eight, with the exposition repeat thrown in for good measure, making for a movement longer than the sum of the other three.

If I understand Schubert rightly, his tempo indication *molto moderato* calls for neither approach. *Moderato* or *mässig*, a term used by Schubert more often than by other composers, seems to imply the calm flow of a measured *allegro*; *molto moderato* would then correspond to a none too dragging *allegretto.* Schubert's avoidance of this word in the B flat Sonata or the first of his Impromptus may be explained by the fact that *allegretto*, like *largo* or *grave*, signifies not only a certain speed but also a certain character. Just like its amiable sound, the word suggests a graceful tripping or strolling. (Moreover, Schubert's first-movement tempo indications refer to the opening; except for the stable *allegro giusto* of the A minor Sonata D.784, the initial tempo of all these movements is modified during the course of the exposition to a more flowing or more measured pace.)

On the question of repeats, let me quote from an article by Antonín Dvořák,[1] which has so far gone unnoticed in the Schubert literature. One of the most affectionate and sensible statements about Schubert, it offers a number of critical insights that appear almost modern. Dvořák, while sharing the view that Schubert sometimes did not know when to stop, writes of the symphonies: 'If the repeats are omitted, a course of which I thoroughly approve, and which indeed is now generally adopted, they are not too long.' Dvořák loved Schubert and knew the classical masters. It would be as silly to accuse him of thoughtlessness or incompetence in questions of form as to accuse Brahms, of whom Edwin Fischer reported:

> How composers themselves sometimes feel about repeats is illuminated by what Johannes Brahms told a young musician who showed surprise that, in a performance conducted by Brahms, the exposition of the Second Symphony was not repeated. 'Formerly,' explained Brahms, 'when the piece was new to the audience, the repeat was necessary; today, the work is so well known that I can go on without it.'

My intention is neither to 'improve' on Schubert nor to abolish repeats altogether. What Dvořák suggested (that Schubert is not too long, provided he is not made longer than

---

[1] Antonín Dvořák (in co-operation with Henry T. Finck), 'Franz Schubert', *The Century Illustrated Monthly Magazine*, New York, 1894

necessary) seems particularly valid in the case of some sonata expositions. Repeat marks should not be taken as a command and obeyed unquestioningly, as if the section had been written out in full by the composer. Before deciding how to proceed, one should consider a number of points:

Does a repeat, within a work or movement, appear necessary, desirable, possible, questionable or harmful?

Was the repeat a concession to those listeners who, conditioned by preclassical dance forms, expected to be led back from the dominant to the tonic – a concession similar to that of incorporating minuets into symphonies and sonatas as an area of repose for sluggish ears?

How extensive is the exposition of a sonata movement, and how tersely or generously laid out is its musical material? (The exposition of Schubert's A major Sonata contains more than twice as many bars as that of Beethoven's 'Appassionata'; it exceeds even that of the 'Hammerklavier' Sonata which, moreover, moves at about twice the speed, while presenting its material at the highest degree of density.)

How far does the exposition differ from the recapitulation? (In Schubert they are usually almost identical. Except for a few significant modulations and transitions, interrupted only by the development, the listener is allowed to wander twice through virtually identical musical landscapes.)

Are the movement's themes distinctly different in character (as is generally the case with Beethoven), or are they intimately connected (as sometimes with Schubert)?

Do the first two movements present a marked contrast (as with Beethoven's Allegro and Adagio), or do they inhabit neighbouring areas of tempo (as often with Schubert's Moderato and Andante)?

What are the consequences of a repeat for the equilibrium of all movements within the work? (In Schubert's last sonatas the final rondos adopt features of sonata form; their symmetrical scheme, with a central development section, seems to me much more happily matched if the first movement repeat is not taken.)

Finally, repeats should be considered in conjunction with

the structure of a whole recital. In the case of a performance of the last three Schubert sonatas in one programme, they are ruled out.

Beethoven's repeats are immediately compelling, with very few exceptions. In Schubert, psychological considerations often overrule formal ones. In music, as with food, quantity can be an important factor. As the British critic Bernard Jacobson has wittily pointed out, both gourmand and gourmet, glutton and restrained epicure, have their musical equivalents. Some musicians seem quite unable to stop making music, unless they fall asleep. Similarly, there are critics – and Jacobson, with admirable candour, counts himself among them – who cannot have enough of a piece they love. I side with the gourmets: my appreciation of food has not been tainted by Marco Ferreri's notorious film *La grande bouffe*, in which a few gentlemen gorge themselves to death. True gourmands avoid seeing it.

The great A major and B flat major Sonatas have stirred the repeat enthusiasts more than other works: did Schubert not write out a few bars which lead back to the beginning? To omit any original music by Schubert, we are told, is unforgivable; it would be equally unjustified to make cuts elsewhere.

I beg to differ. Both expositions end in ways that do not permit a simple return to the beginning. In certain external matters of form and notation, Schubert was much more old-fashioned than Beethoven, and for this reason he wrote down the disputed bars. Beethoven would doubtless have gone straight into the development; in his 'Appassionata' the F minor exposition ends in A flat minor, while the development follows in the unexpected key of E major. It is intriguing to speculate on how Beethoven, with Schubert's harmonic means, might have led back to the F minor of the opening:

Whether in this or any other manner, Beethoven did not see fit to do so. Evidently he was able to resist the pressures of convention where his music called for it.

Another argument advanced by the guardian angels of the B flat Sonata repeat emphasizes the amazing novelty of the transitional bars: they are supposed to add something to the piece which would otherwise remain unsaid, and alter our perception of its character. Even if there were not so many counter-arguments – the generosity of the exposition, the literal recapitulation, the lyric character of all themes (and of the following Andante), the balance between movements – I would, for once, have to disagree with Schubert's judgment. An irrational explosion, such as occurs in the Andante of the A major Sonata, does not come out of the blue. It has its psychological bearing on the bleak melancholy of the movement's opening as well as on the chromatic episodes of the preceding Allegro. But which elements in the B flat Sonata justify the emergence of the transitional bars in question? Where are they announced? Should they be allowed to upset the magnificent coherence of this move- ment, whose motivic material seems quite unrelated to the new syncopated, jerky rhythm? Is the material or atmos- phere of this transition taken up anywhere in the later movements? Should its irate dynamic outburst rob the development's grand dramatic climax of its singularity? Most painful to me, however, is the presentation of the trill in *fortissimo*: an event which elsewhere remains remote and mysterious is here noisily exposed. Schubert's first draft presents the trill, after a relatively brief exposition, in *pianissimo*.

# VI

Schubert could be admirably concise, not only in his *Moments musicaux* and countless songs but also in such a work as the A minor Sonata D.784. I hardly see him among the musical gourmands, anyway. Sketches for his last sonatas show – if one had not surmised it already – how self-critically he proceeded. They also reveal that Schubert's 'length' only appears obsessive where the music is intended to express an obsessive state of mind. In order to move freely, Schubert needs space. In some of his earlier sonatas certain ideas did not receive the ample treatment they deserved. In the sketches for the later sonatas, Schubert's expanding interpolations are particularly convincing. It may be hard to believe, but this is how the lyrical first subject of the A major Sonata appears in the first draft:

Schubert subsequently elaborated on it as follows:

Classical forms define boundaries. The space which Schubert requires in order to move freely has little to do with classical definitions. Haydn did not need such space, although his desire to surprise, his tendency to wander, his naïvety as well as his daring may at times resemble Schubert's. (Haydn springs surprises, while Schubert, I think, allows himself to be surprised.) Mozart's forms give constant evidence of a perfection seemingly without aim or constraint. For Beethoven, form is the triumph of order over chaos, a triumph furthermore of its concord with whatever has to be 'expressed'. Schubert's forms are a matter of propriety, a 'veil of order' – to quote Novalis – which barely conceals the most beautiful chaos music has ever seen.

As early as 1827 the Leipzig *Allgemeine musikalische Zeitung* wrote of the first movement of the G major Sonata that 'within its not unusual formal layout, everything internal [*alles Innere*] is uncustomary and full of fantasy'. Gustav Mahler spoke of Schubert's 'freedom below the surface of convention',[1] and Hans Költzsch, the author of a book which for several decades remained the only (and largely dubious) investigation of Schubert's sonatas,[2] offered the view that Schubert's particular quality as a 'Romantic' lay in his having dissolved the classical legacy from within by preserving much of its outer shell. According to Költzsch, 'isolated deviations from the scheme indicate how far removed the new forces are from tradition', while, at other times, 'the same effect is achieved by an all too schematic compliance with formal usage'.

In his larger forms, Schubert is a wanderer. He likes to move at the edge of the precipice, and does so with the assurance of a sleepwalker. To wander is the Romantic condition; one yields to it enraptured (as in the finale of the A major Sonata), or is driven and plagued by the terror of finding no escape (as in the C minor Sonata). More often than not, happiness is but the surface of despair. Suddenly, the mind is overcast. Nothing is more typical of Schubert than these febrile afflictions of unease and horror, which, in the most extreme case (the second movement of the A major Sonata), hardly attempt to maintain any 'veil of order': apart from its chromatic bass line, the only remnants of organization are a few of those motivic particles common to all three sonatas, which I shall discuss later.

---

[1] 'ungebundene Anlage unterhalb des Üblichen'
[2] *Franz Schubert in seinen Klaviersonaten*, Leipzig, 1927

# VII

Order, even when only an adornment through which the chaos of emotion shines, is decisive because it makes the work of art possible. Such order, however, is never complete. Modern science seems to have moved away from the idea of a rigorous master plan behind the evolution of nature. The concept is no longer that of an engineer strictly realizing a design but of a tinkerer, as François Jacob has suggested, who uses the available components as best he can, mending and combining them, producing intentional or random mutations. The 'natural' process of composition is similar. The composer limits himself to the available basic material, which is usually provided at the beginning of a piece; he sifts, rearranges, varies, develops or comments, with the aid of hypothetical working schemes which leave a small but important area open to chance – and whim.

Among the concepts of order which left an imprint on Schubert's sonatas is that of the interconnection of themes, the cohesion of movements. Just how verifiable is this? The 'inner unity' of a cyclic composition has been much discussed, with rather more reliance on interpretative notions than on evidence provided by the musical material. The first to mention a 'substance common to all movements' was, to my knowledge, Walter Engelsmann (*Beethovens Kompositionspläne*, Augsburg, 1931). According to him, each Beethoven sonata is 'developed from one single principal subject or motif in all its sections'. It is scarcely surprising that Engelsmann did not manage to present convincing proof for his ambitious thesis.

The pipe-dream of a system into which everything can be crammed and by which everything can be evaluated is a temptation analysts can rarely resist; it is all too easy to see what is hardly there while overlooking what should be self-evident. In Rudolph Réti's over-complicated motivic analysis of Beethoven's *Pathétique* Sonata, there is no mention of the significance to all themes of the fourth and fifth, or of their summation as an octave.

Masterpieces never betray all their secrets, not even those of craftsmanship. Invariably, only a few threads are disclosed. It is considerably more profitable to pursue the thread of motivic connections than opinion on the Continent and in the USA would acknowledge. The word 'analysis' is sometimes held to stand for a process of dissolving the whole into its component parts, while it ought in fact to guide us from specific details towards the whole. Long before the advent of twelve-tone technique, motivic and thematic cross-references provided the most unequivocal hallmarks of musical cohesion. When Hans Keller sought to unearth the latent elements of unity in the manifest contrasts of a work, however, I asked myself whether such elements had necessarily to be latent. Is manifest proof of musical unity not widely overlooked? I am not, of course, referring to such patently audible ones as the dotted rhythm of the 'Wanderer' Fantasy, Berlioz's *idée fixe* or those transformations in Liszt and César Franck which leave the notes of a theme easily recognizable while its character changes. (In Liszt's B minor Sonata, the background of Beethovenian motivic relationships is considerably more interesting than the evident metamorphosis of Mephisto into Gretchen.) A hidden connection, says Heraclitus, is stronger than an obvious one (*Fragments*, 54). It is the more subtle motivic coherence which in the long run leaves the deeper mark – provided that a certain measure of musical common sense, a firm ground of verifiable fact, is not abandoned.

# VIII

Let me explain the motivic connections in Beethoven's so-called 'Appassionata'. My awareness of such connections stems from my own experience in dealing with all the Beethoven sonatas, even if my findings tally with some of Réti's. I have gratefully adopted his term 'interversion', a word that signifies those variants of motifs or motivic groups in which only the sequence of notes is changed.

The opening of Beethoven's Sonata Op. 57 (see example overleaf) contains:

1. A (broken) triad;
2. An octave (as octave leap or area or transposition of a phrase);
3. A second as appoggiatura or trill, most frequently in its simplest form of three notes, and in the degree of the dominant;
4. The area of a third, filled in by the combination of the simple trill (C–D–C) with the fast trill (D–E–D);
5. Note repetition.

Of lesser consequence, and not included in this survey, are
the intervals of a fourth and fifth.

The D (D flat) – C of the trill reappears before long as a
'drum-tap' appoggiatura in the bass (3').

**Beginning of 2nd theme**

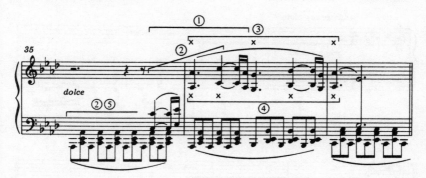

**Beginning of 3rd theme**

Beginning of variation theme

In the further course of the variation theme, the central pitches *db*-*c*-*db* appear as a variant of the 'drum-tap' theme, returning three more times in its second part. (I use the term 'central pitches' for notes which recur prominently throughout the whole work.) The theme's triadic component indicates that the idea of the triad, whether broken or chordal, is a constituent element of the piece; in variations 2 and 3 we find the triad dissolved in figuration.

The larger structure of some themes is permeated by the changing note (3). In bars 3 and 4 of the first subject, the first note can already be heard as the beginning of the changing note, as Schenker and Réti have shown.

The harmonic scheme of the opening

recurs in the third subject as well as in the principal subject of the finale. In the case of the Andante, the Neapolitan harmony is transformed into a subdominant chord with a sixte ajoutée.

In the coda of the finale, what appears to be a new theme is derived from the first subsidiary theme of the first movement or, more precisely, from its reappearance in bars 239–241, linking one stretta with the other.

Not every work proceeds with such rigour. Some are assembled playfully around a principal idea, as is Beethoven's Op. 10 No. 3, which revolves around a short motif with its inversions and interversions.

Other works go back to a number of basic formulas at random or develop new material as they proceed. Groups of works can also be interdependent. Beethoven's last three sonatas (Opp. 109, 110 and 111), for instance, make use of the area of the sixth as a combination of third plus fourth (6 and 6-4 chords). Within this hexachord, steps of thirds and fourths occur more frequently, a succession of six neighbouring notes more rarely, as in the second movement and Arioso of Op. 110. A zigzag of thirds and fourths distinguishes not only the fugue theme but also the beginning of the first movement of Op. 110 (here the left hand assists the right).

Analogously, Var. 5 of Op. 109 features melody and bass together.

Var. 2 already seems to move in Op. 110 territory.

At the beginning of Op. 109, the zigzag of thirds and fourths is similarly evident.

Here the six notes of a hexachord between tonic and third are simultaneously provided by the bass. They characterize the bass line of all principal themes in this sonata.

Another hexachord area is that between G sharp (III) and B (V) in the middle voice. We find it recurring not only in this sonata

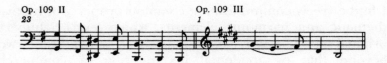

but also figuring prominently in Op. 111.

The fugato theme in the development of Op. 111 offers a chromatic zigzag variant.

# IX

While the composition of Beethoven's Opp. 109, 110 and
111 was spread out over three years (1820–22), that of
another famous trilogy, Mozart's final symphonies, appears
to have been completed in a matter of months (in 1788). In
this respect, and in their musical magnitude, these symphonies are comparable to Schubert's last sonatas. Here the
question arises: what happens when a great composer creates
a series of works virtually side by side? Their individual
characteristics will certainly be strictly defined. But what of
the thematic-motivic material? Is it to be rigorously specified
or will there be give and take? In both Mozart and Schubert
I find a freely communicating common property of motivic,
thematic and harmonic elements, which lends Schubert's
original titles (*Sonate I, Sonate II, Sonate III*) a significance well
beyond that of accidental juxtaposition or commercial
viability. We encounter a family of pieces.

Looking at Mozart's last symphonies, one is struck first of
all by the astonishing similarity of two themes.

It may take longer to realize that both are derived from the
slow introduction of K.543.

This opening contains the same three- or fourfold note repetition which figures in every movement of all three symphonies (more frequently in its threefold form). The beginnings of K.550 and K.551 are likewise infused with the threefold beat.

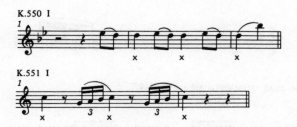

The opening of the 'Jupiter' Symphony offers a premonition of the opening bars of its finale.

This is only one of at least eight statements of these bars within the whole work. In the minuet, the first six notes of the finale theme are stated in retrograde.

The second part of the finale theme (bars 5–8) is anticipated in the trio section of the same minuet

and, most elaborately, in the ten-bar theme of the preceding Adagio.

The first four notes, or more extended portions, of the finale theme already feature frequently in the other two symphonies, as in the second movement of K.550

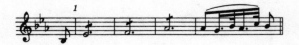

or in the last movement of K.543.

In the first movement of K.543, the opening of the Allegro presents the intitial motif of the 'Jupiter' finale no fewer than three times.

Bars 27–29 introduce another striking familial trait of all three symphonies: the melodic use of the 6-4 chord, often ascending and sometimes, significantly, starting with a leap of a sixth.

Its position is usually in the tonic, less frequently in the subdominant. In the 'Jupiter' Symphony, all principal subjects relate to the subdominant sixth of C major, C–A. The beginning of the G minor Symphony's second movement sounds to my ears like a combination of the 6-4 chord and the initial notes of the 'Jupiter' finale which also appear in the first four bars of the K.551 Adagio as a complement to the melody.

# X

Most of the significant note sequences and note areas in Schubert's sonata trilogy are provided by the first lines of the C minor Sonata (see example overleaf). Like a large quarry, this rugged theme contains building material for future use.[1] Two figures in particular are of far-reaching consequence: those of bars 7/8 (*b*, *c* and example 40) and 14/15 (*h*). The first moves within the compass of a minor sixth, the second within a diminished fifth; I shall refer to them as the *Sixth* and *Fifth formulas*. The first five notes of the Sixth formula (*h'*) are related in retrograde to the Fifth formula (*h*). Both formulas are stressed within the theme by being repeated and varied.

---

[1] On pp. 102–16 I have assembled a series of examples which will demonstrate the motivic coherence of the three works.

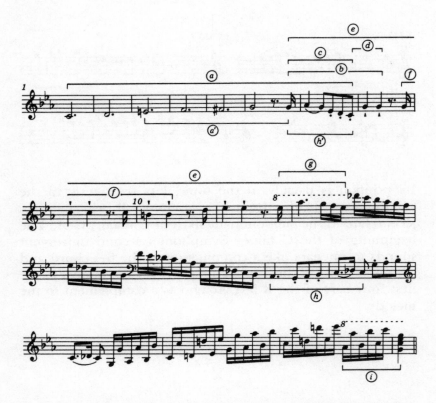

In all three sonatas, formula *h* proves to have the greatest impact. It is taken up in the same key in C minor II[1] (ex. 2). The beginning of the minuet (6), abbreviated by one note and in the minor key, looks back to the lyricism of the Adagio and of the Allegro's second subject. The same note area, as we can see in exx. 4, 6, 7 and 9, can be harmonized in major as well as minor. Exx. 9–13 are distinguished by the same 'A major position', even when located in the B flat Sonata (12, 13).

The G–F appoggiatura in the first subject of the B flat Sonata, which I mentioned above, is ambiguous. It belongs to the middle voice, legitimizing the 18-bar melody of the soprano voice as an extended version of formula *h*. At the

---

[1] For the sake of conciseness, movements are denoted by Roman numerals.

same time, it is an integral part of this melody which, without these two notes, sounds trivial; at the beginning of the scherzo and in the coda of the finale, 'both voices' are thoroughly amalgamated (21, 22). Another amalgamation precedes the third subject of the first movement, following the notes F–G–F with the initial notes of the work, a terse statement of the opening material which clears the way for the new theme (24).

The effect of the beginning of the C minor Sonata (formula *a*, 25) is pursued in exx. 26–34. The opening melody of the finale has its roots in the Sixth formula *b* and its continuation formula *f* (35, 36), if one is willing to accept the workings of interversion. Schubert changed the first two bars twice; the final version comes closer to formula *d*, while the original had varied figures from the first and third movements.

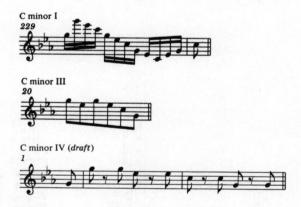

From this opening Schubert had distilled the beginning of the episode, which also takes up the rhythm of the preceding chordal blows.

Along with the plausibility of such motivic relations, the

102

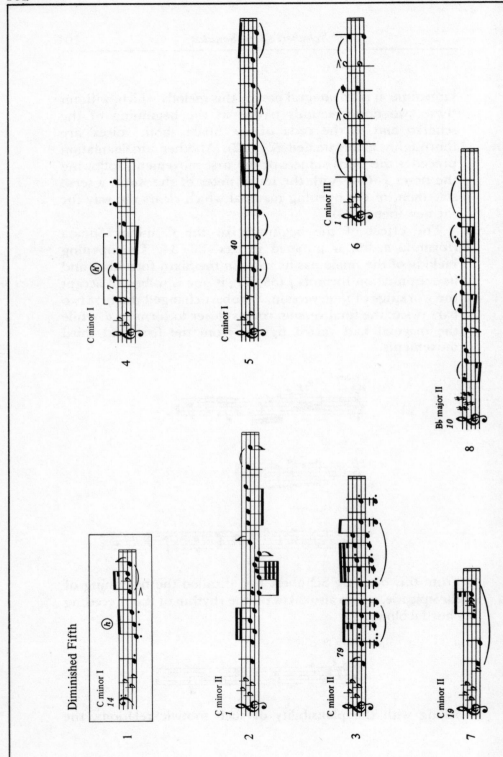

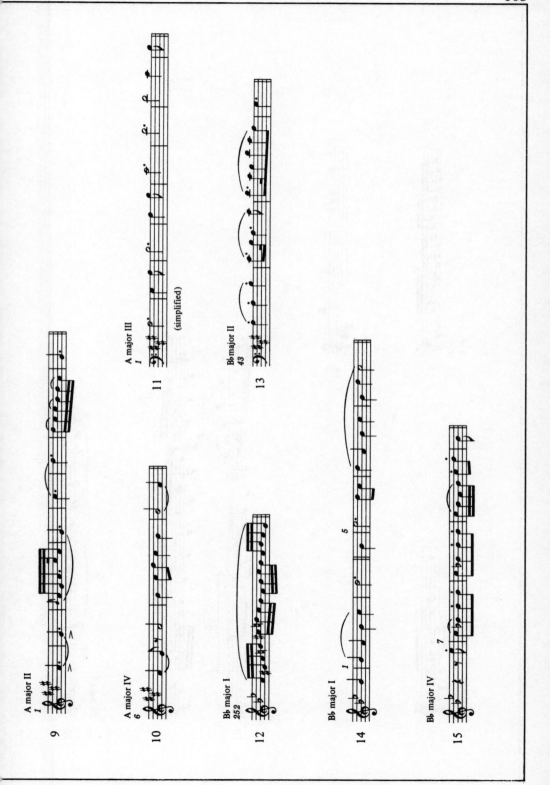

A major II
*1*

9

A major IV
*6*

10

A major III
*1*

11

(simplified)

Bb major I
*252*

12

Bb major II
*43*

13

Bb major I

14

Bb major IV

15

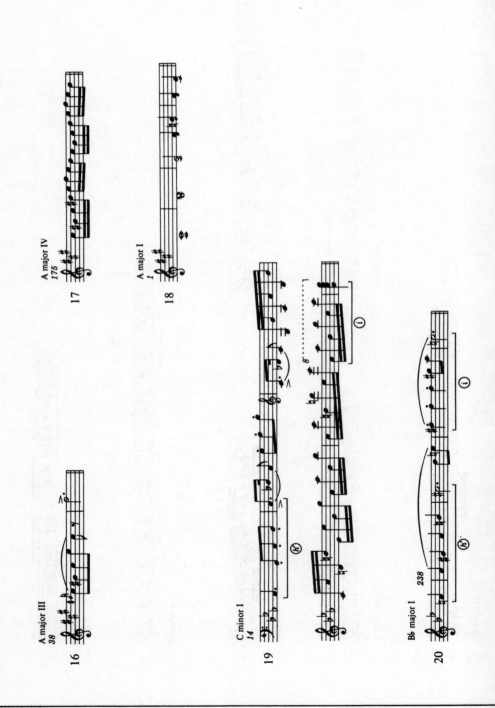

Amalgamation of two voices

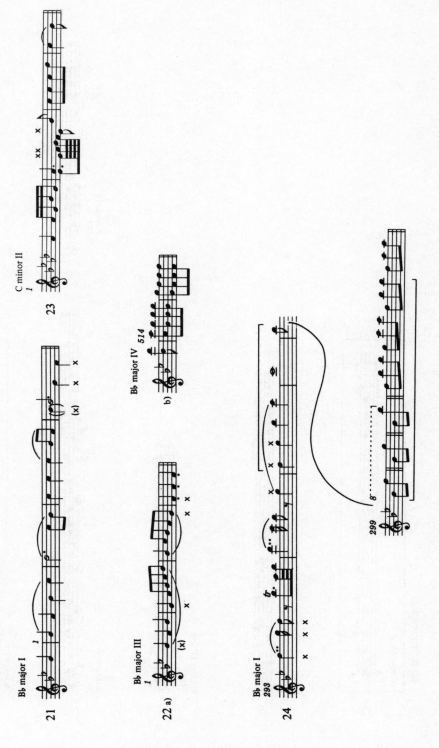

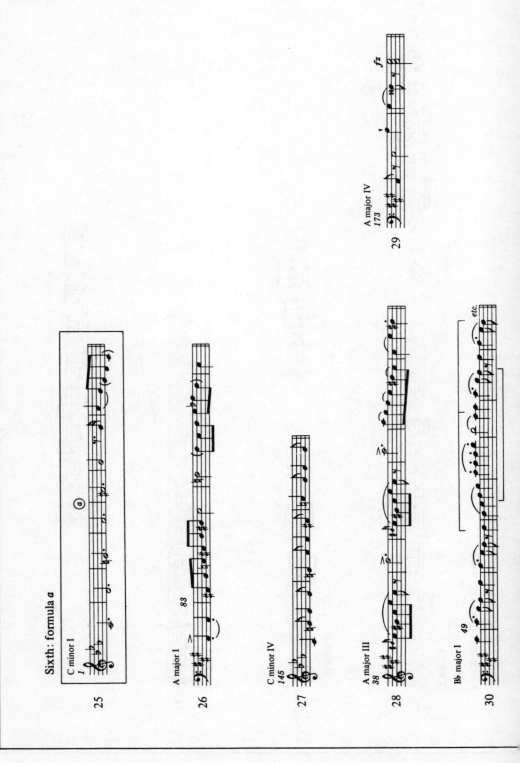

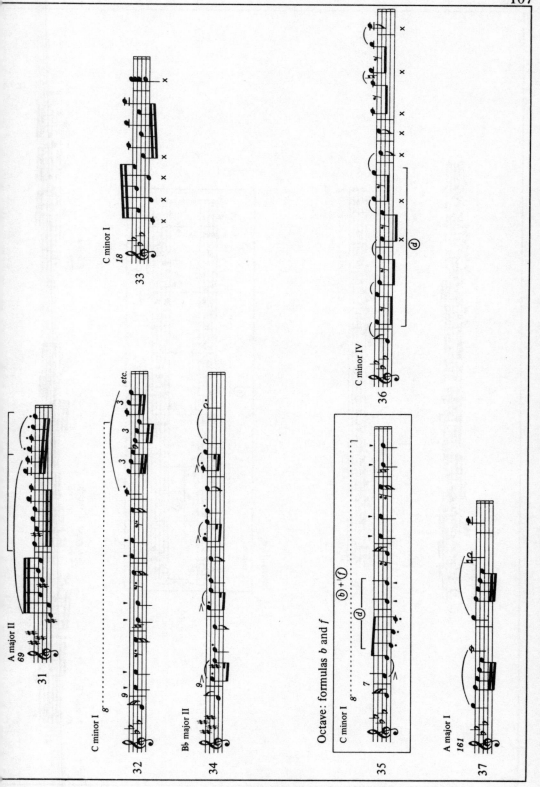

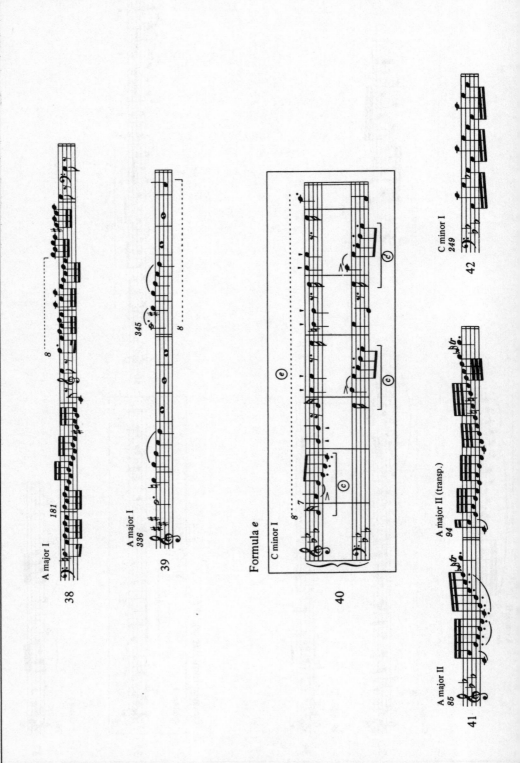

Formula e

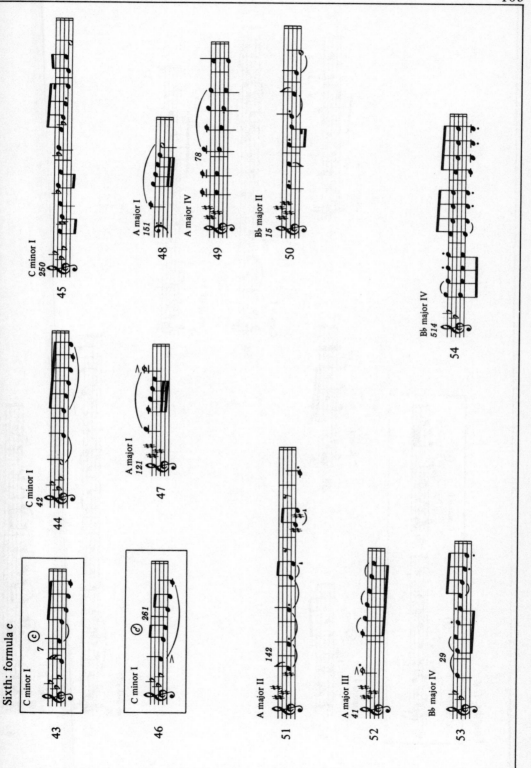

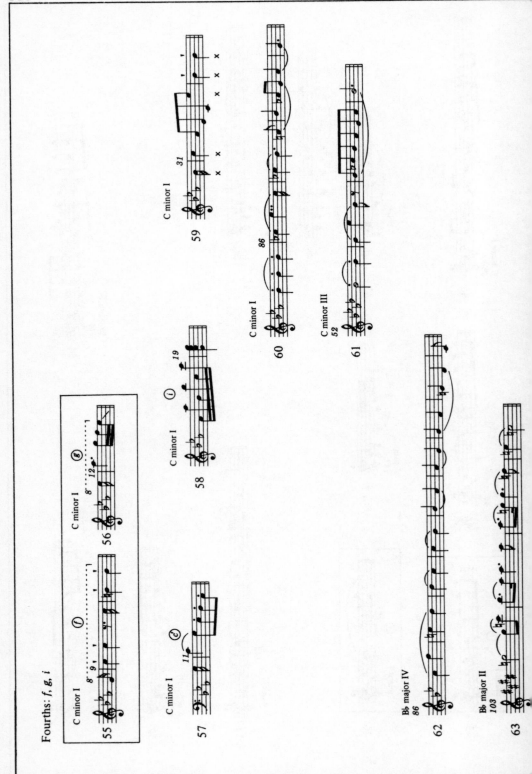

Fourths: *f, g, i*

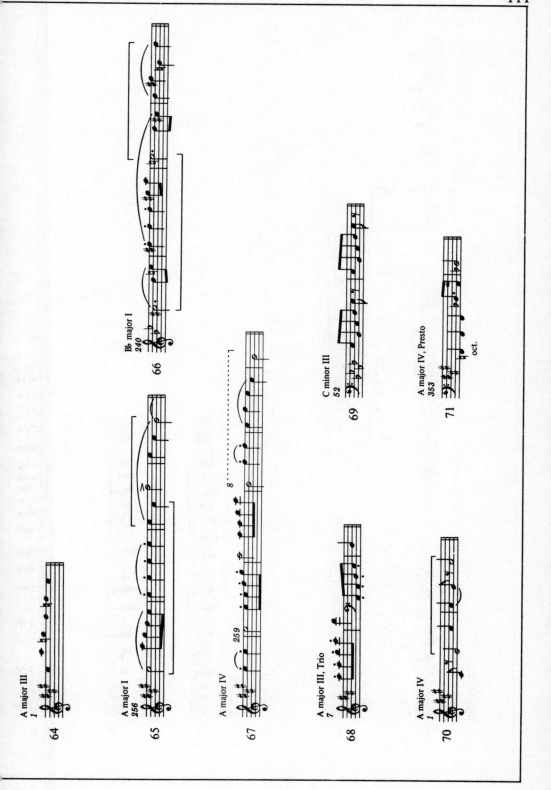

112

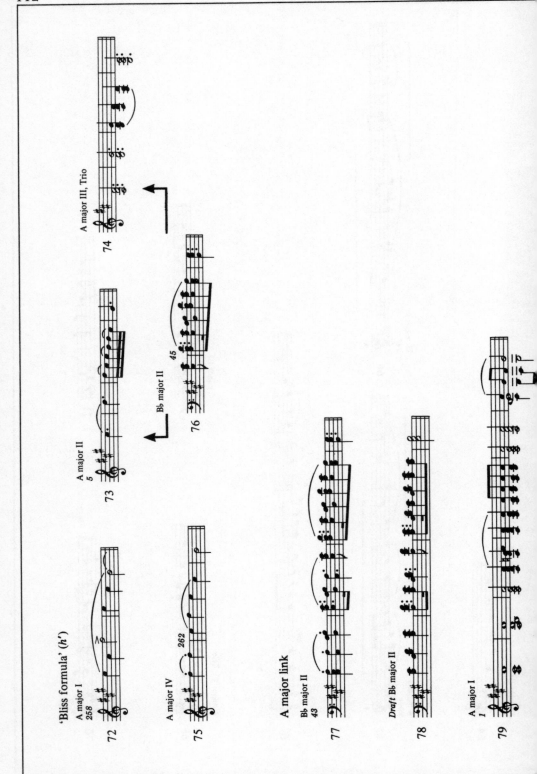

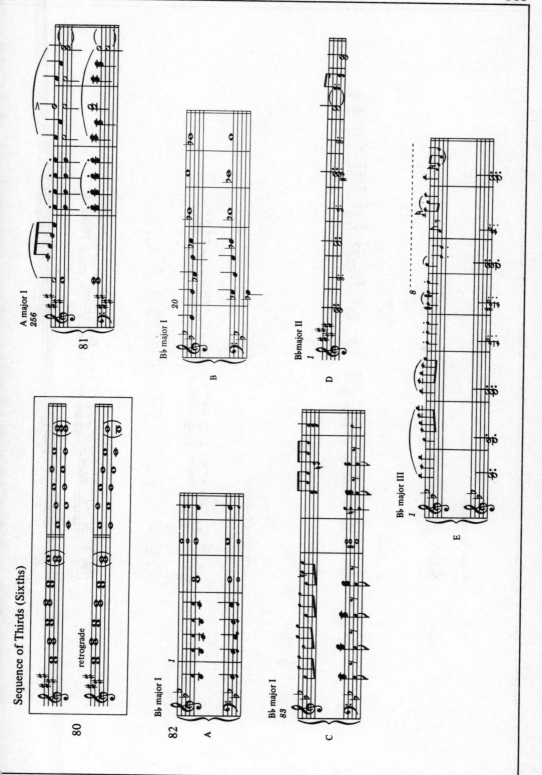

Sequence of Thirds (Sixths)

80

retrograde

A major I
256

81

Bb major I
82

A

Bb major I
83

C

B
Bb major I
20

D
Bb major II
1

E
Bb major III
1

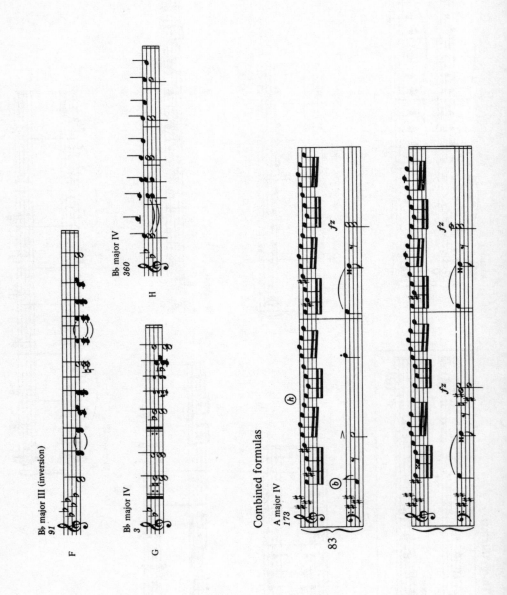

115

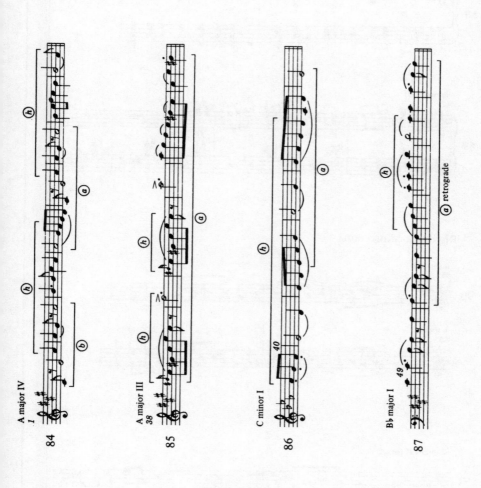

**C ♯(D♭) – F♯ minor link**

C minor IV
113

B♭ major III
47

## Rhythmic connections

A major I
55

A major I
65

C minor II (bass)
1

C minor II
18

(Arthur Godel, p. 162)

harmonic connection of the initial version with the minuet has been lost.

The melody at the end of the episode combines the arpeggio of the movement's original opening with the revised harmony.

Later I shall hint at the psychological cause and effect of Schubert's far-reaching correction.

Examples 35–54 deal with the Sixth formulas *b*, *c* and *d* and their continuations *e* and *f*, a group of motifs which hardly has any bearing on the B flat Sonata. It is remarkable that the F sharp minor Andantino (A major II) points back in its turbulent middle section to the distant key of C minor and the compass of formula *e* (40–42); for a few bars, not only the key but also the character of the C minor Sonata make an impressive appearance.[1]

In ex. 40 a variant of the Sixth formula *c'* (bar 11) now contains the leap of a fourth, as a reaction to the fourth in the melody two bars earlier. Exx. 55–71 concentrate on the *Fourth* motifs contained within the opening of the C minor Sonata (*f*, *g*, *i* and *c'*). The effect of motifs *f* and *g* in particular can be traced in both other sonatas. Ex. 64 simplifies the line of the highest notes in the scherzo theme of the A major Sonata. In exx. 65–67 two elements succeed one another: a lyrical variant of the Fourth formula and,

---

[1] As William Kinderman has pointed out to me, 'one could argue that the shadow of the C minor Sonata is not only cast on the middle section of the Andantino but on the Andantino theme itself, and beyond into the F sharp minor episode of the B flat Sonata'.

derived from *h′*, a figure of unselfconscious bliss between the sixth and second note of the scale which, although a constituent element of the A major Sonata, turns up in the B flat Sonata as well. Even there, the 'bliss formula' reappears in keys of the A major sphere. Within the key of F sharp minor, in A major II, bliss turns into melancholy (73).

Combining features of the A major and B flat major Sonatas, the A major theme in the middle section of B flat major II emerges as a mediating factor between the two works, and as a focal point of motivic orientation within the trilogy. In its melodic sequence of sixths, it comes close to the B flat Sonata's beginning (77). The version in the first draft (78), however, makes it sound very much like the opening of the A major Sonata (79). Clearly, it was this degree of similarity which caused Schubert to reformulate the theme. The version in the draft, as well as the first, purely chordal version of the A major Sonata's beginning, should open our ears to another crucial harmonic-melodic factor common to the three works: the *sequence of Thirds* (or Sixths) (80) which is inherent in nearly all themes, if sometimes modified or latent. The opening of the C minor Sonata is no exception:

Exx. 82 A–G pursue the sequence of Thirds in the themes of the B flat Sonata.

The combination of formulas is examined in exx. 83–86. The fusion of Sixth formulas with the Fifth formula *h* in A major IV may draw our attention to the fact that this theme's innocent predecessor in the second movement of Schubert's Sonata D.537 did not reach down to the third.

The second subject of the B flat Sonata (87) has been placed beneath that of the C minor Sonata (86), as they are related in retrograde.

A *Seconds* formula should be added to the list:

A first hint of it can be discovered in bars 5–7 of the opening of C minor I. The return of the theme brings the variant:

Bars 119–152 of the development are guided entirely by the Seconds formula. From its melodic constellation, harmonic consequences are drawn. There are areas of harmonic twilight: are we in the tonic or the dominant?

In the A major Sonata we encounter the same ambiguity on three occasions.

Here Schubert has taken his cue from the first movement of Beethoven's 'Sonata quasi una fantasia' Op. 27 No. 2.

In B flat major IV the development section is fired by a Seconds formula (bar 256) which had previously brought the first subject brusquely to its close (bars 30–32).

The same formula marks the entire layout of C minor IV: its most important sections begin in the keys of C minor – D flat major (beginning of episode) – B major (middle section) – C minor.

In B flat major III the second subject seems to reach back to C minor IV (exx. 88, 89). Even the keys, C sharp minor (D flat major) – F sharp minor, remain the same. Of these, C sharp minor and D flat major have their say in all three sonatas, whereas F sharp minor and G flat major appear mostly in the C minor and A major Sonatas. A major II is in F sharp minor, B flat major II in C sharp minor.

More easily discernible, and therefore not included in the musical examples, is the *Octave leap*. We find it in bar 4 (ascending melody) and bars 8 and 10 (descending bass) of the C minor opening. It figures prominently in every movement of the A major Sonata but also in C minor IV where, in the initial sketch, the ascending octave dominated much of the movement. It further appears in the episodes of C minor II and, less significantly, in three movements of the B flat Sonata (I, bar 301 and development; II, accompaniment; III, bars 5–8).

## XI

The use of motifs is not generally tied to specific keys. There are some special cases, however, where motifs appear in fixed positions, with or without octave transposition. Such a tone constellation can be noted in exx. 9–13, 20, 30, 77 and 82D; it remains fixed in the A major – F sharp minor sphere within the compass of *g♯-d'* or one octave lower, and is confined to the sonatas in A and B flat major. A first glimpse of this position is provided by C minor II (if such chronological reckoning makes any sense within these works). One of Schubert's most personal modes of expression is his shifting the basic key by a semitone; the appearance of A major in this A flat major movement (bar 56)

is an event whose reverberations remain evident in the coda.

The same Adagio presents, for the first time, a note constellation C sharp – B sharp – E, fixed in C sharp (D flat) minor. We discover it in the bass of the second subject:

Other instances of the C sharp minor constellation can be found in exx. 16, 17 and 34.

The opening of the C minor Sonata includes a succession of chromatic notes (bars 3–7)

which remains effective as the *Chromatic constellation*.

See also ex. 64.

It seems remarkable that, in all three first movements, chromatic developments begin their ascent on the note E.

# XII

'Transgressions' of motivic material are mainly, as in Beethoven, those of note sequences, note areas and note constellations. In comparison with Schubert's preceding sonatas, the significance of rhythmic motifs has diminished. Rhythmic variety is now more important than rhythmic unity.

In the first subjects of C minor I and A major I, as well as in the accompanying figure of B flat major II, there is a unifying rhythmic formula: ♪♩♩ (♪♩♩). The rhythm of C minor IV evolves from its upbeat beginning as a variant at approximately double speed: (♪) ♫♪ ♫♪ etc. B flat major I refers to this rhythm in bars 65/66 and 284/285

(♪♫♫) , while IV dwells on it extensively in its *ff* episode, where the key of F minor mediates between the keys of the two sonatas, B flat major and C minor. (B flat major IV refers to the C minor Sonata in yet another way: it simply insists, as it were, on opening in C minor. It does so, stubbornly, no fewer than nine times; only before the stretta is the C minor spell finally broken.)

A major I derives its main rhythmic impulses from two formulas

(*a*)  ♩ ♩  (on the beat),          (*b*)  ♪♩♪♩

which, in succession, in conjunction or in opposition, steer its course and hold it together. In Schubert's draft, the opening formula *a* was not used from the outset; it surfaces later, during the further course of the exposition, and contributes to the initial chords in the recapitulation. In his fair copy, Schubert added the rhythm by analogy to the very beginning of the work. The first-movement coda, after dwelling exclusively on formula *a*, surprises us with a formula *b* close.

Other rhythmic connections are given in exx. 90 and 91, the latter devised by Arthur Godel.[1]


# XIII

While a basic repertory of note sequences and note areas supplies the majority of themes in the three sonatas (least plausibly in C minor IV), the character of each individual work and movement is set clearly apart. (I believe that, for the player, definition of musical character can be of the greatest value. On pp. 126–7 I have tried to tease out the characters within the trilogy or put my feelings about them into words.)

One could say that the Fifth formula leans towards lyricism, whereas the Sixth formulas are mostly propelled

---

[1] *Schuberts letzte drei Klaviersonaten*, Baden-Baden, 1985

and excited (except the descending formula *e*, which tends to be gentle and lyrical). The Fourth formula is open to both possibilities. Yet if one compares themes of gentle solemnity based on the Fifth formula – the second subject of C minor I and the beginnings of C minor I, B flat major I and II (middle section) – distinct, if discreet, differences of temperament become apparent.

Besides the gentle and solemn, there is a disturbing and menacing side to Schubert's last music. Its classical poise is sometimes undermined by anxiety, exploded by nightmares or shaken by despair. In such moments the music exposes neither passions nor thunderstorms, neither the heat of combat nor the vehemence of heroic exertion, but assaults of fever and delusion. Chromaticism raves in the opening movements of the C minor Sonata (development) and A major Sonata (stretti); the episodes of the Adagios in the C minor Sonata and the String Quintet are darkly affected by fever; the middle section of A major II almost destroys itself in a frenzy of anguish. I shall refrain from connecting such states of mind with the reality of Schubert's illness, something Fritz Lehner, in his fictional Schubert film of 1986, unfortunately did not avoid. Is it not sufficient to feel that, at certain moments in this music, demons descend to strangle or mercilessly to chase? It is precisely the obsessional quality of the C minor finale which makes this movement convincing – in a good performance.

Until recently, Schubert's macabre side has been largely ignored, suppressed or restricted to what was seen as its epitome, 'Der Erlkönig'. Walter Dahms, in his Schubert biography of 1912, found these words for the C minor finale:

> Light-winged, the coquettish six-eight theme flutters upwards. It offers plenty of opportunity for hide-and-seek, and for extensive gossip ... Thanks to the speed with which the changing pictures pass by, one does not notice the movement's length. Suddenly: dominant, tonic, the end.

Taking Dahms's lead, one could perceive 'Der Erlkönig',

| I | II |
|---|---|
| **C minor** | |
| *Allegro* | *Adagio (A flat)* |
| At once heroic and anxious, nervous and determined, threatening and threatened. Sections in major keys (second theme) in parenthesis: vistas of unattainable bliss as seen from harsh, inhospitable surroundings. Coda of despair. | Spiritual, tenderly solemn, devoid of pathos, intermittently gripped by surge of fever. |
| **A major** | |
| *Allegro* | *Andantino (F sharp minor)* |
| Kaleidoscope of ideas and feelings (approximately: 1. Credo, ma con fuoco; 2. Capriccioso con grazia; 3. Dolcissimo innocente; 4. Delirando). Seemingly improvised; in the development section, poised, transfixed stasis, and wide, lyrical-dramatic arch. Mystery coda. | Desolate grace behind which madness hides, from which it erupts, into which i sinks back quivering. Expiring coda. |
| **B flat major** | |
| *Molto moderato* | *Andante sostenuto (C sharp minor)* |
| In its basic character: composed, gently hymnic. Grand musical context that is broken up towards the end of exposition and recapitulation, blissfully fatigued. Coda of humility. | Clear-sighted melancholy, with middle section singing praise. |

| III | IV |
|---|---|
| *Menuetto: Allegro*<br><br>Anti-minuet, at once nervous and determined, without firm ground under its feet. Suburban trio. | *Allegro*<br><br>Dancing dervish; or death gallop, with Cerberus barking, and the B major lure of the Erl King. |
| *Scherzo:*<br>*Allegro vivace*<br><br>High-spirited, frolicsome, with dolce French horns (or male choir) in the trio. | *Rondo: Allegretto*<br><br>The big daydream of bliss, with thunderstorm development, and multifariously fragmented coda: first hesitating, then storming, finally recapitulating. |
| *Scherzo:*<br>*Allegro vivace con delicatezza*<br><br>Soaring, playful. Trio: muffled and obstinate. | *Allegro ma non troppo*<br><br>'Fatigue and resignation'? No, rather: graceful resolution, playful vigour. Ironic twinkle; generous singing line; stubborn pugnacity. Surmounting of C minor fixation after the ninth assault: precious moment of self-abandonment. Assertive coda. |

without the corrective of its text, as a cheerful gymnastic exercise. According to Költzsch, the C minor finale reveals 'simple technical incompetence' and offers 'little more than rhythmic sound-motion'. As for the A major Sonata's Andantino, he asks himself whether 'the strangely eruptive caprices' of its middle section might not be 'partly artificial'.

Arthur Godel has described the main section of this Andantino as a 'peaceful barcarole' and the C minor finale as 'moderate', devoid of any 'manic dimension ... The playfully and generously unfolded C minor theme with its optimistic brightening into the major (bar 67 etc.) lacks the vehemence of syncopated accents and the awkward minor-major alternation of the G major Quartet's finale.' This may be so but, given the restriction of its comparative monotony, the movement manages to be all the more tortuous. As mentioned above, Schubert altered the first two bars of the initial theme; by eliminating the onslaught of its broken chord, which had dominated large portions of the movement in the manner of an *idée fixe*, and by providing a necessary minimum of melodic variety (at the expense of reducing the logic of motivic cohesion), he prevented the monotony from becoming unbearable.

In contrast to Dahms, to whom the C minor finale is 'light-winged', and Godel, who finds it intermittently optimistic, the composer Dieter Schnebel detects in the comparatively light-hearted finale of the B flat Sonata 'strength that peters out – an ominous image of impending death ... For the time being, cheerful music no longer seems to work – it may not ever again.' According to Schnebel, the whole movement represents a 'hidden diminuendo', containing 'musical symbols which anticipate Mahler in the hammer strokes of his Sixth'. In the first movement of the B flat Sonata, where Dahms made out a 'flowering, momentous main theme' and 'genial lyricism', Schnebel sees the 'document of a disintegrating life'.

I feel little inclination to quarrel with a man of such stimulating intelligence, but there is no option. Is it impossible to imagine that Schubert, even as a sick man, might have been able to convey in his music emotions of well-being, teasing, excitement, euphoria, a happiness conjured up by his imagination (if not founded on fact) which would try to ease what he called his 'dismal awareness of a miserable reality'? Is it not likely that a depressive composer, instead of letting himself sink deeper into despair, would take advantage of the act of composing as a lever with which to lift himself out of his inertia? Is it frivolous to conceive that even a syphilitic may have some light-hearted notions a few months before he dies? Where Schubert was once labelled genial and sentimental, he has recently been construed as desolate and relentlessly depressive. The protagonist of *Lilac Time* wreaks belated vengeance, while the aura of what had been termed 'Schubert's last compositions' adds a shiver of awe. In the A major Sonata's finale, Schubert sounds joyfully transported; in the scherzo I hear laughter and see hats thrown into the air. The 'optimistic' episodes of the C minor finale, on the other hand, turn out to be chimeras, insinuations of the Erl King.

# XIV

Comparison between fair copies and first drafts reveals a change in Schubert's perception of musical space. In the sketches, certain ideas or sections are already laid out in their entirety, while others appear all too condensed; only in the revision are they given the space they deserve. Such a flowering of the original seed provides an amazing glimpse into the workings of an imagination at once fertile and critical. Proportions are rectified, details start to tell, fermatas suspend time. Rests clarify the structure, allowing breathing space, holding the breath or listening into silence. (In the sketch, C minor II contains not a single fermata, the minuet not a single bar's rest!) Some ornaments are added, others deleted, such as the trill on E in the third bar of the C minor Sonata, or the turn between C sharp and D in bar 49 of the A

major scherzo. Where ruggedness is moderated, the music is
not weakened but clarified. Occasionally Schubert takes a
risk which he felt compelled to tone down in the final
version: I note with regret that in bar 73 of A major II he
softened the staggering G major chord by turning it into a G
sharp appoggiatura.

This G major harmony communicated at one stroke the
hallucinatory quality of the new section, and initiated the
pedal G that gives support to the following twelve bars before
being resolved into C minor. Significantly, this movement
assembles all three dark keys – F sharp minor, C minor and,
at the climax of the central section, C sharp minor – as the
utmost concentration of the trilogy's depressive forces.

# XV

Portraits of Schubert, it seems to me, often show him idealized, as if trying to produce a face harmless enough to match the sounds of *Rosamunde*. A more realistic Schubert is presented by the 1826 portrait without glasses (Gesellschaft der Musikfreunde, Vienna) and particularly by the life-mask, copies of which are preserved at the Curtis Institute in Philadelphia and the Vienna Conservatory.[1] This mask, evidently suppressed by Schubert's friends, has at last received due recognition, thanks to the efforts of Eva Badura-Skoda.[2] (I agree with her assumption that it can hardly be a death-mask, as which it was previously identified.) What we see is not a 'Biedermeier face' but powerful, sensuous, robust and propulsively energetic features, more akin to those of Beethoven than to Grillparzer's or Johann Nestroy's. Similarly, the musical image of an idealized, harmonious Schubert has long determined the taste of performers and listeners. Even today, he remains for some largely a source of lyrical, genial, mellow and elegiac pleasure. The 'well-known timidity and phlegm' ascribed to him by Schindler is unhesitatingly applied to the character of his works. (According to the recollections of Schubert's friends, he was far less timid than Schindler made him out to be; and what could be phlegmatic about the temperament of a man who produced nearly a thousand compositions in a short lifetime?)

'A gentle melancholy pervades Schubert's music,' writes Godel (p. 254). The crisp enthusiasm of the Great C major Symphony, the vitality of many a scherzo, the fury of certain finales, the acute despair of *Winterreise*, the terror of 'Der Doppelgänger' are all as far removed from gentleness as Goya is from Schubert's Viennese painter friends. Kupelwieser or Schwind never painted the equivalent of what

---

[1] Reproduced in the entry on Schubert in *The New Grove Dictionary of Music and Musicians*

[2] Eva Badura-Skoda: 'Eine authentische Porträt-Plastik Schuberts', *Österreichische Musikzeitschrift*, November 1978

Schubert called his 'gruesome songs'. To be sure, Schubert, that most immediately moving of all composers, offers beside his chill dances of death also something of the warmth and shelter of death, its sweetness and enticement, its siren voices and lure to surrender. After the death of his mother, her memory seems to have merged into an image of death. But here as well the word 'gentle' will not do. The singer who observes the dynamic markings of *Winterreise* (written predominantly in the piano part) will be bound to startle those listeners who consider an evenly beautiful sound and a nobly shaped phrase the quintessence of lieder singing, and *Winterreise* the musical portrait of a resigned old man.

Schubert's dynamic markings are extreme, indeed far more so than those of Beethoven. (The same applies to his daring harmony, with his fondness for juxtaposing chromatically neighbouring keys.) Experience teaches the player, however, that Schubert's dynamics are frequently incomplete; he tends to omit intermediate steps, as for instance in bars 184–224 of the B flat finale: literally, a decrescendo is supposed to begin after nineteen bars of pianissimo, followed eight bars later by another decrescendo which after four bars, in its turn, leads into a diminuendo that prevails for the last eight bars. Even as an idea, this hardly makes musical sense. Schubert evidently left it to the player to take corrective action, such as starting each phrase (upbeats to bars 202, 210, 216) at a slightly stronger dynamic level. In his notation Schubert takes too much for granted: I wonder whether he ever had the opportunity of hearing his piano works played by others, and of reacting to performances.

Another source of misunderstanding is Schubert's use of accents. In his autographs they vary considerably in size and graphic emphasis, so that an accent may sometimes look like a diminuendo. (The new Bärenreiter complete Schubert edition simplifies the problem unduly: instead of adhering as closely as possible to Schubert's own ambiguity, leaving decisions to the player, a very small accent has frequently been used.) On the keyboard the matter is particularly precarious. Schubert's mania for accents calls for discretion;

otherwise the pianist may sound pedantic and run the risk of over-emphasizing isolated notes in cantabile. In recent years Schubert's old-fashioned triplet notation has justly received some publicity. Here I should like to correct myself and announce that, in the Adagio of the C minor Sonata, I have now come to adjust the dotted octave leaps (bar 32 etc.) as well – a long look at the autograph (Floersheim Collection, Basle) has taught me that polyrhythm seems out of the question. In his fair copy, Schubert replaces the single dots of his sketch with double dots, a fact which serves as an argument for, not against, adjusting the triplets: only the shorter rhythmic value may be adjusted.

For yet another reason, examination of Schubert's autographs proves essential: his use of ties is casual, incomplete and sometimes indecisive. I have come to treat such ties in secondary voices *ad libitum*, following my ear.

# XVI

Three quotations from the Schubert literature:

His pianistic style is demanding enough, even sometimes in his songs. But it hardly goes beyond Beethoven in the exploration of technical possibilities, and would seem to have been determined by the light touch and bright tone of the Viennese instrument of his period.
(Hans Gal, *Franz Schubert and the Essence of Melody*, 1974)

Little tension, but an even sweetness and a deficiency of tempo.
(Carl Spitteler, *Schuberts Klaviersonaten*, 1887)

The permanence of the theme as a theme is guaranteed in the potpourri, adding one theme after the other without having to draw consequences from any modification ...

assortment of themes blindly embarked on . . . Just as there
is no constitutive history between the entry of one
Schubertian subject and the next, life is not an intentional
object of his music.

(Theodor W. Adorno, *Schubert*, 1928)

A musicologist-composer in the most conservative mould, a
music-loving Swiss poet and a composing thinker offer
statements that need to be questioned.

Schubert's piano style is by no means that of Beethoven; in
its part-writing and disposition of sound, it seems to me often
fundamentally different, while its rapid octaves, tremolos
and note repetitions prepare the way for Liszt. To me,
Schubert's piano style is determined far more by vocal and
orchestral colour than by the timbre of contemporary
Viennese keyboard instruments. The influence of string
quartet or quintet sonority is as evident in his last sonatas as
that of his sacred choral music. Only a number of his lyrical
piano pieces (Impromptus, etc.) show a more directly
'pianistic' approach, and only there should the player's inner
ear immediately imagine piano sound.

It is easy to deduce from Spitteler's comment that he had
never heard good performances of the Schubert sonatas. It is
to his credit that he paid heed to them at a time when nobody
else seemed to care.

As for Adorno, his assumptions about the 'potpourri'
nature of Schubert's music, its random arrangement of
beautiful themes without inner connection or development,
do not bear scrutiny. After introducing the second subject in
F sharp minor in the first movement of his B flat Sonata – a
theme which Adorno cites as an example of unrelatedness –
Schubert leads up to the third subject with a twenty-bar
motivic development. The area of the sixth inhabited by the
F sharp minor theme (ex. 87) is modified to that of a
diminished fifth.

The next step brings out elements of the first subject.

Finally, from a shorthand version of the first subject, the third subject emerges (ex. 24).

The highly unorthodox first movement of the A major Sonata begins with two successive, heterogeneous ideas. I have tentatively called them 'Credo, ma con fuoco' (bars 1–7) and 'Capriccioso con grazia' (bars 7–16). They immediately begin to interact (bars 16–22). The second idea is propelled through an extensive development, arriving at the third, the actual subsidiary theme (bar 55), which is itself intimately related to the beginning of the piece: the initial harmonies are now supplied with a cantabile melody in the soprano. Again there is no sign of an abrupt change of scenery. The music which follows the subsidiary section, growing out of its final rhythm, could easily be taken for the actual development section. (The unwitting listener expects it to lead into the recapitulation and may, indeed, have the erroneous impression that it has arrived there – if the player does not skip the repeat.) In contrast to this exposition full of development, the beginning of the actual development section seems to suspend time and activity; it is a product of the exposition's codetta, generously laid out in cantabile style, a variant of 66. Later on, the Credo character, with its octave leaps, gradually takes the lead, preparing the entry of the recapitulation with symphonic grandeur.

Potpourri-like exposition, interchangeability of themes, developments lacking in conflict – these are much less Schubert's than Mozart's hallmarks. In the exposition of the Piano Concerto K.595 Mozart presents an array of at least eight different melodic sections, in the manner of an 'unending melody', and seemingly without any constructive commitment. The result is phenomenal and seamless.

# XVII

Of Schubert's last three sonatas, the one in B flat has, in our century, cast the strongest spell. One could call it the most beautiful and moving, the most resigned and harmoniously balanced, corresponding most clearly to the concept of a gently melancholic Schubert.

The first two movements sound valedictory. Farewells are not necessarily composed in the face of impending death. Beethoven had a penchant for farewells far beyond his 'Lebewohl' Sonata: from the Andante favori to the Adagio of Op. 111 and the final minuet of the Diabelli Variations, 'Lebewohl' pervades some of his codas, both in the sound of its syllables and as an emotional hue.

Everything in the B flat Sonata seems controlled and considered. The F sharp minor theme that so startled Adorno, far from appearing out of the blue, has its harmonic and motivic roots in the lines which come before, while the aggressive episodes of the finale are preceded by a silence of the kind that anticipates the storm. Only those transitional bars in the first movement, an intrusion from the feverish regions of the other two sonatas, ignore the newly acquired countenance. Carried over from an earlier phase of conception, they seem to me no less ill-advised than the execution of the repeat which they instigate.

If the B flat Sonata is the most beautiful, the one in A major must be the most astonishing and remarkable. Here, the brightest of worlds confronts its darkest counterpart. Between movements which, luminously, bring together certitude and adventurous flight of fancy, sweetness and mystery, wit and abandon, stillness and chromatic uproar, stands the Andantino, spelling out the most acute emotional disturbance. The first movement maintains a precarious balance between improvisation and construction, operating with changing degrees of weight, varying its narrative pace and disclosing only with hindsight the highly unusual formal scheme. The coda quotes the movement's initial idea in a different light: not with confident timpani strokes but in a whisper; not in public but in secret. Its final arpeggios combine elements of both initial characters – broken chord and octave leap – in reverse direction, descending, no longer ascending. The first pianist to give the sonata its due was Artur Schnabel. Even today, his 1937 recording transmits the freshness of an exhilarating discovery.

Seekers after comforting musical beauty will be taken aback by the C minor Sonata; predominantly sombre, passionate yet icy, it may well be the most unsensual, uninviting and, behind its classical façade, the most neurotic sonata Schubert wrote.

Schubert helped to carry Beethoven's coffin. One year later, he evokes the memory of Beethoven and the classical style, but is no docile follower. On the contrary, his familiarity with Beethoven's works taught him to be different. Dvořák noticed that Schubert had from the outset little in common with Beethoven except 'in the vigour and melodious flow of his basses', already found in his early symphonies.

The idea that Schubert tried to model his sonatas on Beethoven's and failed has nevertheless confused many a listener; all the more so in the earliest decades of this century, when it became fashionable to break away from the pathos and musical idealism of Beethoven. In 1927 Maurice Ravel explained Beethoven's fame as resulting mainly from his deafness, from the legend of his life, and from the magnanimity of his social ideas! Neoclassicism, 'Neue Sachlichkeit' and protest against the dominance of 'German' instrumental music combined to belittle not only Beethoven's but also some of Schubert's achievements.

Arnold Schoenberg knew better. In a short text drafted for the centenary of Schubert's birth[1] he emphasizes Schubert's 'inconceivably great originality in every single detail next to a crushing figure like Beethoven', which has either remained unnoticed or been denied. No wonder this originality was not fully appreciated, even at a time when its

---

[1] The Schoenberg Institute, Los Angeles

boldness had almost ceased to be disturbing. Schoenberg's admiration for Schubert's 'self-respect' is boundless: 'Close to such crushing genius, Schubert does not feel the need to deny its greatness in order somehow to endure. What self-confidence, what truly aristocratic awareness of one's own rank which respects the equal in the other!'

Schubert relates to Beethoven, he reacts to him, but he follows him hardly at all. Similarities of motif, texture or formal pattern never obscure Schubert's own voice. Models are concealed, transformed, surpassed.

Beethoven's influence on the finale of Schubert's great A major Sonata is hidden (or would have remained so but for Charles Rosen and Edward Cone), although the movement adheres to the formal example of Beethoven's Op. 31 No. 1 finale. Schubert's C minor Sonata seems more overtly Beethovenian in its key, its character of sombre determination, its sublime Adagio which replaces the usual graceful Andante, and in the contribution of sonata form to its rondo. There are also thematic resemblances; for instance, the theme of Beethoven's C minor Variations seems to have triggered off the opening of the Schubert C minor Sonata. However, while Beethoven organizes his theme within the stringent logic of 'foreshortening', Schubert allows his foreshortenings to go astray. The character Beethoven presents is one of defiance based on firmness of musical proportion. Schubert presents an energy that is nervous and unsettled, avoiding four- and eight-bar patterns; his pathos is steeped in fear.

The player who, at the beginning of the A flat Adagio from the C minor Sonata, is reminded of Beethoven's Op. 10 No. 1 Adagio or, rhythmically closer, of the Largo from Beethoven's C major Concerto, should be aware of the different emotional situation: where Beethoven offers tenderly enraptured declarations of love, Schubert embarks on his movement in 'holy sobriety' (*heilignüchtern*, to borrow Hölderlin's word). The emotional climate of the D flat theme (see p. 122) is thoroughly modified in comparison with the first subject of the Adagio cantabile of Beethoven's *Pathétique*, from which it may be derived. A second glance at the Adagio and the minuet – an anti-minuet in the manner of Haydn – reveals that these movements owe more to Haydn than to Beethoven, and to the string quartet more than to pianistic predecessors. (The fingers of every pianist will have noticed that the finale also incorporates some ideas which could be more painlessly executed with the string bow.) Schubert's Adagio seems in spirit to be only a small, albeit highly personal, step removed from the slow movement of Haydn's B flat Quartet Op. 76 No. 4. We easily forget that the solemn Adagio – also that of earlier Beethoven – originated in Haydn, and that the first of all great C minor piano sonatas was Haydn's. Even more perfunctory are reminiscences of Beethoven's Op. 31 Nos. 2 and 3 in Schubert's C minor finale, the controlled frenzy of which adopts a novel, almost pathological course.

Schubert's last sonatas belong together. A succession of musical examples – mostly beginnings of themes – should make this even more obvious. The examples are arranged as a chain of developing variations and transposed, where necessary, into the same A major/F sharp minor range, to facilitate comparison (see pp. 140–1). Another chart shows (simplified) melodic connections in the two inner movements, both within the same work and in relation to the other sonatas. Not that the three works cannot be played separately; yet, as they illuminate one another, they seem to me more interdependent than Beethoven's sonata trilogies. A thesis of menace and destructive energy (C minor), followed by an antithesis of positive, luminous activity (A major), is concluded by a synthesis of resigned composure. The finale of the B flat Sonata shows a kind of gaiety that is neither innocent, like that of the 'Trout' Quintet, nor teethgnashing, as in the finale of the String Quintet. Its territory lies somewhere between the humour of Jean Paul and the well-known Viennese saying that life is 'hopeless but not serious'. It is comforting to know that the composer of *Winterreise* should have been able, shortly before his death, to make light of his suffering. Nothing, however, could reconcile us to the cynicism of a fate which was to take his life away at the age of thirty-one.

*(1988)*

Succession of examples — mostly beginnings of themes — from Schubert's last three sonatas, arranged as a chain of developing variations, and presented within the same A major/F sharp minor range, starting with the Fifth formula (*h*).

Melodic connections in Schubert's last three sonatas
(second and third movements)

# Testing the Grown-up Player: Schumann's 'Kinderszenen'

'Easy pieces for the pianoforte' – what Schumann himself presented as easy, simple and childlike proves to be, for the performer, a trying task. In this music nothing can be concealed. Each note must speak with its particular significance, neither taken too lightly nor buried in 'meaning'. There seems to be a prevailing attitude in performances of Schumann's *Scenes of Childhood* which, if I had to put it in one sentence, would read: 'As naïvety cannot be forced, let us improvise and trust in God.' The results of such trust can be deplorable. What these miniatures need is affectionate care, loving detachment, an appearance of directness. The player should not turn himself into a child.

Where the artist mobilizes childlike qualities in himself he does so with artistic means to serve his artistic purpose. Alban Berg censured Hans Pfitzner for seeing in 'Träumerei' the prime example of 'inspiration', a melody sent down from heaven, rendering the analyst speechless. In Berg's brilliant account of the compositional process of 'Träumerei', its motivic connections with other pieces in the cycle are not discussed. Before I try to deal with these connections, let me examine another area that links the pieces.

Over a few weeks during February and March 1838, Schumann composed 'nigh on thirty quaint little things', thirteen of which he put together as *Scenes of Childhood*. In this arrangement a magnetic cohesion seems to have taken hold of the pieces, pointing out relationships, and turning them into components of a lyrical world bigger than the sum of its parts.

Among performers, perceiving series of pieces as a complete whole is a relatively recent notion. Busoni seems to have been one of the first pianists to play Chopin's Preludes and Etudes complete. Liszt, in his Leipzig performance of *Carnaval*, restricted himself to a selection of the pieces, and

Clara Schumann in the same work simply left out 'Florestan', 'Eusebius' and 'Chiarina' – too intimately connected with her private life, according to Tovey.

Of the *Scenes of Childhood*, 'Träumerei' has achieved notoriety around the globe. I remember a villa in Buenos Aires which bore the inscription 'Reverie'; it fulfilled the promise of its name by providing a musical-box performance of 'Träumerei' while the visitor entered the house. Standing on its own, the mauled piece seems to have changed its identity: it is strangely different from those thirty-two bars that occupy the central position (No. 7) in *Kinderszenen*. There, after the comic excitement of 'Wichtige Begebenheit' (Important Event), 'Träumerei' comes as a surprise in F major, an island of peace, a small domain of suspended breath and intangibly dislocated rhythmic emphasis, a delicately polyphonic dream, before the lively motion of 'Am Kamin' (By the Fireside) transfers the listener back to reality.

Within the whole course of *Kinderszenen*, 'Träumerei' is the first, crucial turning-point. The reign of sharps during the first six pieces, in keys gathered around D major, has now been broken; only the next turning-point, No. 10, will bring them back. Here G sharp minor abruptly follows the C major close of 'Ritter vom Steckenpferd' (Knight of the Hobby-horse, No. 9) – an event gently introduced yet traumatic in its impact. The new emotional state – ironically intimated by the title 'Fast zu ernst' (Almost too serious) – is maintained in all the remaining pieces. It manifests itself as nervous sensitivity in the increased complication and irregularity of musical phrases; as the inner unrest of syncopations and fermatas in 'Fast zu ernst'; and as wavering between E minor and G major in 'Fürchtenmachen' (Frightening) – which, in spite of its soothing G major ending, remains rooted in its parallel E minor: the next piece, 'Kind im Einschlummern' (Child Falling Asleep), makes this evident. But here again the conclusion is not on the tonic E minor on which the piece started, more awake than asleep; it stops on a wonderful, truly romantic A minor chord that opens up like a mouth opened by sleep.

This mouth, to pursue the analogy, now begins to speak
with the voice of the poet. In the last piece, 'Der Dichter
spricht', the poet speaks an epilogue, and answers the
unresolved A minor question by leading back into the initial
key of *Kinderszenen*, G major. We have come full circle: while
in the preceding pieces the poet had seemingly turned into a
child, the epilogue turns the child, as it were, into the poet.

A cycle of smaller pieces challenges the performer to
reconcile two points of view: the acute characterization of the
single piece and the pull of the whole. Cortot's recording of
Chopin's Preludes is a perfect model. In it each prelude
instantaneously shows its own, unmistakable face. One
follows the other almost without interruption, a credit to
Cortot's truly phenomenal command of character. The fact
that each piece inhabits its own world, and the voyage
through all the keys, become hallmarks of the Preludes'
organization. In other cycles, constant looking back to the
theme (variation form) or the common denominator of
motifs may tie the complete work together. Usually in cyclical
works the momentum of musical events is such that a quiet
intake of breath between pieces is a rare occurrence. In
*Kinderszenen* tiny separations before 'Träumerei' and after
'Fast zu ernst' are required. All the other pieces should lead
into, or follow, one another without pause.

## *Motivic Connections*

As usual, the very beginning presents the crucial motivic
material. (My reference to the lovely opening phrase of the
first piece as 'motivic material' will offend only those who
believe that poetry and intellect are opposites; Romantic
aesthetics should show them otherwise.)

The *basic motif*

**Von fremden Ländern und Menschen**
(Of Foreign Lands and People)

reappears in the pieces that follow in a variety of shapes, always related to the notes of the melody but not to its rhythm. These notes are B – G – F sharp – E – D; we find them plain or in disguise, transposed or untransposed, varied in their order of succession (which Rudolph Réti[1] calls 'interversion') or provided with additional notes ('auskomponiert', to use Schenker's term). Two shapes of the basic motif may be distinguished by name. In the *Original* (OR) our motif recurs on its initial pitch independent of key – regardless of octave transpositions or added accidentals. The *Transposition* (TR) puts the initial notes into different keys and/or different degrees of the scale.

From an ample number of examples, I should like to offer the following selection.

In the openings of the second and third pieces there is an interaction between TR and OR.

**Kuriose Geschichte** (A Droll Story)

**Hasche-Mann** (Catch me if you can)

The fourth piece, 'Bittendes Kind' (Entreating Child), has the OR, without any melodic change in the key of D major.

After various transpositions in the fifth piece, the OR appears at its conclusion:

---

[1] In Réti's *The Thematic Process in Music* (Faber, 1961) *Kinderszenen* is presented as a 'theme with variations'. This seems to me to exaggerate the closeness of its pieces. As so often, Réti gets carried away by the notion of a near-complete motivic coherence. The results of my own independent investigation are, I think, more modest.

**Glückes genug** (Happy enough)

The beginning of the sixth piece combines two transpositions:

**Wichtige Begebenheit** (Important Event)

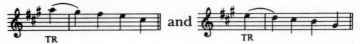

Its middle section distributes the TR

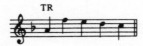

between two figures:

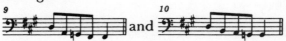

In the theme of 'Träumerei' the TR is easily audible.

The eighth piece contains, next to transposed interversions of the basic motif, the OR twice.

**Am Kamin** (By the Fireside)

In the first four bars of the ninth piece there is a TR in the background.

**Ritter vom Steckenpferd** (Knight of the Hobby-horse)

With the tenth piece the situation becomes more complex. The change of emotional climate has its motivic implications.

**Fast zu ernst** (Almost too serious)

TR (interversion)

Starting with the two G sharps in bars 1 and 3, I hear their continuation in the fifth bar.

The figure returns very similarly later on.

At the beginning of the eleventh piece there is, again, an opportunity to 'listen ahead'.

**Fürchtenmachen** (Frightening)

A later version of the OR reads:

The penultimate piece distributes the OR between two voices.

**Kind im Einschlummern** (Child Falling Asleep)

OR

In the last piece the perspective has changed. The basic motif almost disappears. Four-note fragments can be spotted in the initial phrase and, somewhat more distinctly, in the recitativo, while the complete transpositions are barely noticeable.

**Der Dichter spricht (The Poet Speaks)**

Here the player should observe the part-writing with loving care; the ascent of the G sharp up to the E of the appoggiatura can easily remain obscure. I am still waiting for the edition that will visually clarify the matter and refrain from printing that last note of the turn underneath the anticipated E. Where Schumann's notation errs, we are entitled to correct it. The entry of the appoggiatura, by the way, has to coincide with the C of the bass if the ascending interval of the sixth is to become clearly audible. In bars 18 and 23 we can detect two intertwined transpositions in the upper voice and one in the middle voice. Whether, and to what degree, such motivic procedures are produced intentionally is open to speculation. To me, devices of musical order are no less impressive if generated, or adopted, by the workings of the unconscious.

## Metronome Figures. A Digression

In *Kinderszenen* Schumann makes do without conventional tempo indications, although he elsewhere, whether in German or Italian, invariably adheres to them. Instead there are descriptive titles — 'of course devised later', as Schumann explains, 'and actually nothing more than subtle hints at performance and conception' — as well as metronome marks.

The latter are contained only in subsequent editions of the first print, which has none. Malcolm Frager kindly told me about a copy of this *Urtext* of all *Urtexts* (in the Staatsbibliothek, East Berlin) in which its owner, a certain Otto Boehme, had written: 'The metronomes of *Kinderszenen* are neither by Schumann nor made with his knowledge and assistance ... I got this information from the music dealer Friedrich Whistling of Leipzig (13.9.46), who in turn got it from Schumann himself.'

On the other hand, there is a comment by Brahms which refers to the preparation of a complete edition of Schumann's works (Breitkopf & Härtel); in a letter to Clara Schumann of April 1879, Brahms writes: 'Notify Härtels that the pedal and metronome markings in *Kinderszenen* have to remain. The volume delivered to me shows that Schumann himself owned such copies and had them bound.' (Brahms's advice was not taken.) When we look at Mr Boehme's own insane metronome figure for 'Träumerei', $\downarrow = 132$, we can quickly disregard him as a musical authority – unless he has mistaken quavers for crotchets. Whether authentic or not, I feel obliged to examine Schumann's 'original' metronomes and try to make sense of them.

I confess that I am more comfortable with the *idea* of a tempo, even if rather vaguely expressed by words like 'allegro' or 'andante', 'sehr rasch' or 'mässig', than with the outstretched finger of the metronomic prescription. Is the information conveyed by a figure really more precise? Does a minutely described fictional character come to life more vividly than one that leaves enough room for the imagination to fill in the details? I have met only one musician who possessed the equivalent of absolute pitch, an absolute memory for tempo. The ability of the late conductor Paul Paray to reproduce, and retain, a certain tempo evening after evening seemed unfailing even at the age of ninety. Other musical mortals, composers not excluded, are prone to considerable fluctuations in their perception of tempo, owing to hall, instrument, weather, and well-being. (I shall not consider here the practice of modifying an initial tempo.)

The player or listener may have very different memories of performances of the same piece, even if the stopwatch guaranteed that the duration was identical to the second; what dragged along yesterday seems fluent enough today. Otto Klemperer in his old age hardly realized how slow his tempi were and how much they had slowed down since his earlier years. Béla Bartók, one of the most meticulous masters of notation, attended rehearsals of his works with the pocket metronome on alert, yet played in his commercial record three of the four movements of his Suite Op. 14 at least twenty beats faster than he himself had stipulated. And how embarrassing for conductors to learn after thirty-five years that the printed metronome figure for the second movement of Bartók's Concerto for Orchestra – desperately adhered to against their better judgment – reflected the composer's wish as little as did the verbal tempo indication (Allegretto scherzando ♩ = 74, instead of the authentic Allegro scherzando ♩ = 94). According to Leonard Stein, Schoenberg's assistant in Los Angeles, Schoenberg's as well as Stravinsky's notions of tempo varied greatly over the years. In Schoenberg's Piano Concerto Op. 42, judging by Eduard Steuermann's performances, some metronome marks are 'correct' while others, ignored by Steuermann, are absurd and unplayable. On a tape of a performance by Steuermann and Hermann Scherchen (Frankfurt, 1955) the work lasts nineteen minutes and not twenty-eight – the preposterous figure put down by Schoenberg. A literal execution of Schoenberg's metronome indications would render it even quicker.

The 'right tempo', fixed in figures, is hardly the key to the 'right' performance. Rather, the tempo will be a result of all factors combined: the formal and emotional attributes of the composition; its markings which, to a certain extent, regulate articulation, dynamics, character and atmosphere; the descriptive and programmatic indications, if at hand; the (at least approximate) playability; and, finally, the necessary degree of clarity and transparency within the acoustic surroundings of a concert hall.

That said, I should point out that I am not the sort of performer who would disregard the composer's metronome marks untested 'because they don't work anyway'. I am already quite pleased if some of them sometimes do. In the case of *Kinderszenen* I do find a majority of the early metronomes convincing; I adhere to them, at least approximately, in nine out of the thirteen pieces. (Users of the Clara Schumann edition should realize that the metronomes offered in it, which rarely tally with the earlier ones, are of Clara's own invention.) The quick tempo of 'Hasche-Mann' (♩ = 138) is more than justified by bars 15/16: here the sforzando octave in the bass has to be sustained by the pedal, which, if this were done in Clara's ♩ = 120, would produce a clumsy blot. Equally indispensable is a fluent pace for 'Bittendes Kind' if one wants to take the ritards in bars 9–12 seriously. (Clara surpassed herself in reducing the 'original' ♪ = 138 to ♪ = 88!) In 'Wichtige Begebenheit' as well, ♩ = 138 seems to me nearer the mark than Clara's ♩ = 120, which makes the middle section sound unduly pompous. When children come to relay some important news, they rush in and blurt it out.

The lively tempo of 'Am Kamin' (♩ = 138, slowed down by Clara to ♩ = 108) appears to me, after 'Träumerei', just right; instead of dozing off in a corner we enjoy the glowing fire, and manage to get the natural feel of the little retards in bars 16 and 22. Technically, a well-oiled player is needed to execute jumps, accents and polyphony with elegance.

One of Clara's most wilful infringements is her correction, in 'Fast zu ernst', of ♩ = 69 to ♪ = 104. Nothing could be less appropriate than to measure the pulse in quavers. Even Schumann's crotchets appear to be an inadequate solution in a piece whose extended phrases reach over several bar-lines, and steer towards its closing pause. (However, it is only at the repeat of this piece that I approach ♩ = 69, a tempo too agitated for its beginning.) The fluency of 'Fürchtenmachen' is also welcome: instead of an amiable idyll with scary episodes, a character is at once presented whose very timidity makes it liable to succumb to fright.

Four of the 'original' metronome figures have remained, to me, thoroughly implausible. The speed of the first piece, 'Von fremden Ländern und Menschen' (to which, in a rare feat of unanimity, Clara also subscribes), makes it scurry along with the industry of an ant; there is no time to relate to, take in or marvel at anything those unfamiliar shores may have to offer. (According to her best-known pupil, Carl Friedberg, Clara Schumann took it considerably more slowly in performance.) Equally mysterious remains $\downarrow = 100$ for 'Träumerei'. I am the last person to want this piece to reel in pink-and-purple affectation, or collapse under the weight of its own 'depth'. But even Clara's $\downarrow = 80$ sounds hurried and superficial. The cycle's centrepiece and heart deserves better. In 'Kind im Einschlummern' the feverish speed of $\downarrow = 92$ does not permit the child to breathe quietly. (Here Clara's $\downarrow$ = 80 is preferable.) And the poet ('Der Dichter spricht', $\downarrow =$ 112) is prevented, even at Clara's more moderate pace ($\downarrow =$ 92), from accommodating the turns and syncopations of his epilogue poetically. My own approximate tempi for these pieces are: 'Von fremden Ländern und Menschen' $\downarrow = 76$; 'Träumerei' $\downarrow = 69$; Kind im Einschlummern' $\downarrow = 72$; 'Der Dichter spricht' $\downarrow = 82$.

## Irony. A Brief Epilogue

'Glückes genug' – a title that ironically contradicts the music. What happens in this composition rather reminds me of the line from the Swiss poet Conrad Ferdinand Meyer: 'Enough can never ever satisfy' ('Genug kann nie und nimmermehr genügen'). Ceaselessly, the same motivic symbol of rapture reappears in all voices. And there is more to follow: a da capo of the entire piece. But even boundless happiness can overreach itself – within that da capo, I insist on skipping the repeat.

Irony creates distance. In *Kinderszenen* there is an ironic distance between the child and the grown-up in ourselves. We do not identify with the child, and do not want to be hurtful. Schumann's irony in this work is lovingly lenient. With Schumann we observe how a sheltered world turns vulnerable, or 'fast zu ernst', as he put it. If, in irony, things are not what they seem to be, and do not mean what they seem to say, then 'Fast zu ernst', by its title and its music, strips the mask from an illusory security. With irony, we look back to 'Glückes genug'. What appeared naïve proves to be, in Schiller's distinction, sentimental. The Romantic humour of Jean Paul and his disciple Schumann betrays its dark core.

*(1981)*

# The Noble Liszt

Do composers gain from posthumous anniversaries? If their greatness is well enough established, the playing of their lesser-known works may further enhance their reputation; if unduly neglected, they may be helped out of their oblivion. Those afflicted by a history of chronic misrepresentation, pervasive malice and lingering doubt stand the slimmest chance. Celebrating the 100th anniversary of Liszt's death and the 175th of his birth, a plethora of Liszt festivals, marathons and competitions may well prove to have further obscured the stature of a man who has to be defended on several fronts: against some of his champions and partisan admirers, against the crowd of sceptics and adversaries, and, to a lesser extent, against himself.

When Liszt died, he made the mistake of leaving behind an unusual legacy of envy. There is a relation between envy and posthumous fame. Liszt's early European success as virtuoso and improviser equalled that of Mozart; a few years later, his 'genius of expression' (Schumann) and boundless pianistic skill made him, as a player, superior even to Chopin, Mendelssohn or Clara Schumann. The combination of a lively mind, personal magnetism, masculine beauty, the social triumphs enjoyed by a privileged parvenu, and a love life bordering on scandal turned out to be, within one human being, barely forgivable. There was a conspicuous absence of mitigating circumstances, such as Mozart's or Schubert's early death, Mozart's alleged impoverishment and 'unmarked pauper's grave', Schubert's syphilis, Beethoven's deafness, Chopin's consumption, or Schumann's mental disorder – features that make the fame of a genius a great deal more gratifying, and guarantee its solidity. (Wagner's monstrous egotism and merciless promotion of his own ends, while not stimulating compassion or malicious glee, present a frame of mind many people enjoy sharing.)

154

Arguably, Liszt and Haydn are the most frequently misunderstood among major composers; their biographies afford little food for pity. (The insufferable bigotry of Haydn's wife and the senility of his last years do not, it seems, sufficiently atone for his achievement in being the first great symphonist and the grand masterr of the string quartet.) In old age, Haydn reigned over the musical world as its undisputed leading light. For this, the nineteenth century punished him – as it punished Liszt for his undisputed supremacy as a performer. Haydn was branded the ingenuous classicist (something he rarely was), 'the family friend who is always welcome but has nothing to say that is new' (Schumann). Liszt, in his compositions, was seen as a poseur and charlatan (which he only occasionally was), the embodiment of a superficial and bombastic romanticism. Not until our century did a greater number of composers – from Richard Strauss, Ravel and Busoni to Schoenberg, Bartók and Boulez – appreciate Liszt by taking him seriously.

One of the more interesting recent German contributions to Liszt scholarship is the belated publication of Lina Ramann's *Lisztiana* (1895),[1] a collection of reminiscences by Liszt's official biographer. 'Alas,' exclaims Miss Ramann after listening to some of Liszt's classes, 'none of our masters is so dependent on performances that make sense of their compositions ... and only too few players manage to get through to the core of his music! There is a lack of either poetry or intelligence, or wealth of feeling.' In Liszt's case, performance is less a matter of quality than of existence: a 'to be or not to be' of a work, its spark of life. Possibly Liszt entrusted his musical executants with too much power; his demands upon them reflect the transcendent authority of the greatest performing musician of his day.

Most leading pianists of the later nineteenth century had been, at least briefly, among Liszt's disciples; yet, despite all

---

[1] Published by Schott (Mainz, 1983)

claims to the contrary, no convincing tradition of Liszt
playing developed. Of course Liszt, after his virtuoso years,
hardly ever performed his own works himself, and did very
little to promote them. (Rather, he helped others, notably
Wagner.) In the *Liszt-Pädagogium*, a valuable set of comments
on the performance of some of Liszt's works by his pupils,
recently republished by Breitkopf & Härtel, the editor, again
Lina Ramann, counters certain misconceptions about Liszt's
style. According to Miss Ramann, Liszt should be taken as a
lyrical tone poet first and foremost – as a rhetorician,
rhapsodist and mime. The poetic essence of a piece explains
its form, the musical spirit creates its technique.

But poetic freedom is not, 'as the practice of immature
virtuosos may suggest, distortion of form', nor is it 'auton-
omy of virtuoso fingers'. The *grosse Stil* (grand style) becomes
possible only through Liszt's 'periodic execution' that prevails over bar-lines and metric stereotypes. The *melos*, or
melodic spirit, in Liszt no less than in Wagner, permeates
everything; it contains Liszt's 'profundity [*Innerlichkeit*] and
passion' – which brings us to qualities that, alongside the
grand style, should be mandatory for Liszt players. Passion
and introspection, daring and nobility by no means exclude
one another. Nobility need not be pale or academic. Neither
should passion have to be vulgar. Miss Ramann warns against
mistaking 'passage-work' for an invitation to technical bravura, and stresses the importance of rests and pauses – a
point later taken up by Busoni in his *Outline of a New Aesthetic
of Music* – telling us they may be of 'longer or shorter
duration' (than their written value) and have to be determined 'precisely by the character of each transition'.


For Liszt, the much-maligned programme musician, music
was fundamentally a tool of poetic expression, and the piano
an object to be transformed into an orchestra, turned into
the elements, lifted into the spheres. In lesser hands, his
extraordinary pianistic demands risk becoming an end in
themselves. Chopin's strictly pianistic music provided the

ideal medium for a concept of sound that limits itself to a certain idea of beauty, and specializes in maintaining the most ravishing timbre. In Liszt's piano style, the concept of a 'beautiful' sound is superseded by that of an expressive one. Subservient to the desire to encompass every facet of experience, and freed from classical restrictions, the piano is made to release the whole gamut of colour, dynamics and nuance, and encouraged to forget its own boundaries.

Liszt's 'poetic' imagination relied no less on the sensations of the surrounding world than on those of the world within. Their musical transmission is often amazingly subtle and precise – a feat the performer should demonstrate to his audience, and himself. Those who conceive music as 'absolute' and autonomous should find plenty to admire in Liszt's B minor Sonata, the one major work that makes do without any programme or motto; but, even here, they will lose a large domain of Lisztian expression. Without its poetic core, Liszt's music easily degenerates into a vehicle of *Effekt*, which, in its German sense, has been defined as 'effect without cause' by Wagner. On the other hand, it would be a grave mistake to overlook, or underestimate, Liszt's musical intellect even if it was not always employed to full advantage. In the end, response to poetic images may come more easily to many than the insight into Liszt's professional mastery of part-writing (often dissolved in figuration), and the coherence of the musical whole.

Liszt's music, unlike that of Mozart, projects the man. With rare immediacy, it gives away the character of the composer as well as the musical probity of his executant. Hans von Bülow, Liszt's favourite pupil and the first pianist to offer a complete Liszt recital, taught his students to distinguish between *Gefühl* (feeling) and *Dusel* (giddiness, sentimentality). Likewise, one might add, the Liszt player should keep pathos and *Schwulst* (pomposity) firmly apart. When playing Liszt's superb variations on Bach's 'Weinen, Klagen, Sorgen, Zagen', he or she should make the music weep, lament, worry and despair without lapsing into howling, or chattering of teeth, and, at the work's conclusion, whether a believer or not, prove capable of demonstrating certainty of faith without producing a wrong gesture. To a good mime, nothing should be unattainable.


'Good taste is a barrier to an understanding and appreciation of the nineteenth century,' writes Charles Rosen. For Busoni, who stunned Berlin audiences with his series of Liszt recitals in 1905, feeling had to be linked to taste, and style. According to him, the popular concept of feeling ignores taste, and therefore relishes sentimentality and over-projection. In the matter of taste, no composer could be more vulnerable than Liszt. In contrast to Charles Rosen ('To comprehend Liszt's greatness one needs a suspension of distaste, a momentary renunciation of musical scruples'),[1] I consider it a principal task of the Liszt player to cultivate such scruples, and distil the essence of Liszt's nobility. This obligation is linked to the privilege of choosing from Liszt's enormous output works that offer both originality and finish, generosity and control, dignity and fire. Where Liszt has been casual and uncritical, the player, and listener, must come to his rescue. After eliminating many a lesser piece, there still remains a rich harvest, at least within his piano music. It is bound to include his Sonata, the *Années de pèlerinage*, the 'Weinen, Klagen' variations, late pieces like *Mosonyi Mihály*, and a selection from the Etudes – works I feel to be on a par with the best of Chopin and Schumann.

Though enjoying, once in a while, some of the Hungarian Rhapsodies and operatic paraphrases, I wince at Charles Rosen's assertion that 'only a view of Liszt that places the Second Hungarian Rhapsody in the centre of his work will do him justice', or at the kind of praise he gives to Liszt's *Réminiscences de Don Juan*:

With his international reputation for erotic conquest already set, Liszt must have known that the public would

[1] 'The New Sound of Liszt', *The New York Review* (12 April 1984)

take his fantasy as a self-portrait, just as everyone had assumed that Byron's *Don Juan* was an autobiography. As Mozart, in *The Magic Flute*, had used coloratura brilliance as a metaphor for rage and power, so Liszt uses virtuosity here as a representation of sexual domination.

Once again virtuosity and sexuality are in the spotlight. With such distinguished support, the argument whether Liszt's niche should be in the pantheon or in a bazaar of oddities and monstrosities may well drag on.

It is difficult to find, for Liszt's music, a fitting national identity. In the end, not even Hungary laid claim to it after Liszt made the mistake of equating the native folklore of his country with gypsy music. Instead of 'specializing in himself', Liszt presents a panorama of style. His skill in appropriation resembles that of his beloved gypsies. Already the intellectual poets of German romanticism had half adopted, half created a manner of folk poetry; and later nineteenth-century architects made unhesitating use of past styles. Not until Stravinsky, however, did another composer emerge who elaborated on the most varied musical material without losing himself.

Liszt's variety extends from the sacred to the utterly profane, from the lavishly sumptuous to the ascetic – and from the careless to the masterly. His music was deemed lacking in 'Germanity' as long as instrumental music was taken to be a German monopoly. For European purists of the twentieth century, on the other hand, only original compositions were admissible until recently, and preferably those which avoided rhetoric, apotheoses and arpeggios. While much of Liszt's music assimilates material from elsewhere, the use he makes of it is not uniformly felicitous. Melodies by his operatic contemporaries, folk tunes and Gregorian chant lend themselves more readily to Liszt's handling than does Mozart's or Schubert's idiom; this is not a question of Mozart's or Schubert's tunes being too good for Liszt but of Liszt's treatment clashing, to my ears, painfully with their style and character. (An exception is Schubert's 'Wanderer' Fantasy, which Liszt understood well enough; here his error was to 'set free', in an orchestral score, qualities that are supposed to turn the piano itself into an orchestra.)[1] These days, arrangements have regained respectability. If Liszt, however, had left nothing but his lied transcriptions and operatic paraphrases, he would hardly be better remembered than his erstwhile rival Thalberg.

It is upon some of his original compositions that his fame most durably rests. To deny Liszt a melodic style of his own would be unfair, even if the quality of its invention wavers. (Among Liszt's occasional shortcomings are facile melody, the compulsion to say something two or three times, lack of formal economy, and a reliance on the glorious and idealistic.) The B minor Sonata shows none of his weaknesses: none of the themes is disappointing, patterns of repeated phrases help to articulate the structure, the grand design is impressively controlled, and the projected fortissimo ending has been replaced by a moving and mysterious lyrical coda. Altogether, this is the most satisfying sonata written after Beethoven and Schubert, two of the three composers Liszt most ardently admired. (The third, at least in Liszt's earlier years, was Weber.) It has remained the only one of Liszt's large-scale works that, to the last bar, shows him in complete command; all the others, whether orchestral or vocal, suffer, if intermittently, from a lack of economy, direction, thematic distinction, or freshness. (Liszt was not, like Busoni, a natural orchestrator unless he used his own instrument as an orchestra; and he is, to me, more convincing in some of his religious piano pieces – a genre he created – than in his church music.)

---

[1] Liszt's *partitions de piano*, his straight piano transcriptions of orchestral scores such as Beethoven's symphonies or Weber's overtures, are an entirely different matter; what they require from the player is not a 'Lisztification' of style but a faithful reproduction, as far as the piano permits, of their original orchestral colour.

Liszt's works show various degrees of finish. Some were published in several versions; in others, optional variants (*ossias*) testify to restlessness and indecision. In the case of the Transcendental Studies and many pieces from the *Années de pèlerinage* (a few have remained unaltered), the final versions are almost invariably the most satisfying. It was one of Liszt's great achievements during his Weimar years to have made some of his potentially finest compositions playable, if only by a few, and to have clarified their musical purpose. Sometimes a new version amounted to a new piece. The player may permit himself, here and there, to adopt a detail from an earlier version as long as it fits into the definitive one without altering its formal design.

In the only version of his B minor Sonata, Liszt has achieved the same practical clarity of notation that we have learned to respect in Beethoven or Brahms. It is a myth that Liszt needs the kind of extemporizing performer he himself is known to have been on occasion. But was he really, as Harold C. Schonberg maintains, invariably bored if he could not prove his alertness by adding something to the pieces he played? Even if this were so, he would be better served by ardent, if critical, devotion than by performers pretending to be another Liszt. Some of his improvised *ossias* can be attributed to a lack of practice time; his activities as composer, virtuoso, conductor, teacher, writer of essays and letters, reader, lover, society figure, supporter of colleagues, abbé, tireless traveller, whist player, and cigar and cognac addict make it evident that he must have been used to either sight-reading or relying on his memory.

Liszt would surely have been the first to object to others meddling with his texts unless he had given the player an *ad libitum* authorization, as in the cadenza of his Second Rhapsody. (One wonders what he would have made of Horowitz's recorded performance of 'Vallée d'Obermann' which, among various changes, omits several bars of its stormy middle section.) In his *Memories of Liszt* (1877) Alexander Borodin writes:

In spite of having heard so much, and frequently, about his playing, I was surprised by its simplicity, sobriety and severity; primness, affectation, and anything that aims only at surface effects, is completely absent. His tempi are moderate; he does not push them or become hot-headed. Nevertheless, there is inexhaustible energy, passion, enthusiasm and fire. The tone is round, full and strong; the clarity, richness and variety of nuance is marvellous.

Liszt's supposedly arbitrary handling of the music of others is uncorroborated by his editions of Beethoven's concertos, and Beethoven's and Schubert's sonatas,[1] while his pupils hardly dared to touch up his own texts, so that obvious writing or printing mistakes have lingered on to this day. As Liszt confessed, he was a good proof-reader where others were concerned but a bad one for himself.

Modern chroniclers of the piano like to call Liszt a showman. That he was capable of behaving ostentatiously during the most hectic years of his virtuoso career, throwing his kid gloves to the floor of the stage, and staring at the ladies while playing, is undeniable. As a general characterization of his art and personality, however, the label is undeserved. Liszt was the first to depart from the salon. To the displeasure of some contemporaries, he democratized the concert by occasionally performing for an audience of thousands in large theatres like Milan's La Scala. This required a different projection of music, one based on a physically freer and more demonstrative treatment of the piano that, when we take account of the feeble instruments of the 1830s and 1840s, may well have gone through three pianos during one evening. He also inaugurated the 'recital', a concert pre-

---

[1] The sonatas by Weber, however, are a different matter; in Liszt's questionable elaboration of these works, his own promise that the large print would reproduce Weber's authentic text while all of Liszt's additions would appear in small print, was not kept. I counted nearly a hundred errors and changes in the large print of the first movement of the A flat Sonata alone.

sented by one single player, and was promptly castigated for his self-sufficiency.

The personal life of Liszt, like that of Paganini, soon became the subject of myth and calumny. Neither his alleged noble origin nor the 'evidence' of his unofficial children bears scrutiny. Liszt inhabited a world peopled by women writers and fascinated by *romans à clef*. George Sand and Marie d'Agoult parted company over private indiscretions revealed in Balzac's *Béatrix*. The Countess d'Agoult, under the pen-name Daniel Stern, then gave vent to her resentment against Liszt in her novel *Nélida*; in the guise of a painter, Liszt is accused of being unable to produce works in a large format, a charge he once and for all refuted with his B minor Sonata a few years later.

The pinnacle of malice was reached by Olga Janina who, as we are told by Dezsö Legány and Alan Walker, was neither a countess nor a Cossack but a pathological impostor. It is significant that Ernest Newman, the respected biographer of Wagner, was taken in by her books because they represent Liszt, in accordance with his own view, as a weak character. If Liszt was thought in the English-speaking world – at least until the publication of his letters to the Baroness Meyendorff (1979) – 'to be vain, duplicitous and, above all, a showman, given to the tawdry and bombastic in life as in art' (Robert Craft), this was due mainly to Newman's *The Man Liszt*, a book ungenerous to the point of defamation while always priding itself on its 'objectivity'. It was, to Robert Craft,[1] a 'complete and welcome surprise' that Liszt emerged from the Meyendorff correspondence as genuinely modest, sincere in his religious convictions, commonsensical, wise, and full of understanding of human nature. Newman's distorted portrait rests on his musical scepticism: where access to Liszt's music is clouded by prejudice, or lack of sympathy, the outline of Liszt's personality easily becomes shaped according to the writer's distrust. Eduard Hanslick, Vienna's ruling critic, was a remarkable exception: he

---

[1] 'The New Liszt', *The New York Review* (5 February 1981)

esteemed Liszt highly as a man and as a performer, although
he despised his compositions.


During his lifetime, Liszt must have had his portrait painted
more frequently than any other celebrity in Europe. In a new
pictorial and documentary biography that should for many
years set a standard for accuracy and splendour (Ernst
Burger, *Franz Liszt*, List Verlag, Munich, 1986), an oil sketch
shows him being painted by three painters at once. But
Liszt's vanity was counterbalanced by his selflessness, his urge
to dominate held in check by his humility. Has there been
another musician as generously helpful, as magnanimously
appreciative? Liszt bore the *amertume de cœur* (bitterness of
heart), the personal and artistic disappointments of his later
years, with imposing self-control. He mustered the strength
to react against the hysteria surrounding a triumphant
virtuoso career by leaving the concert platform at the age of
thirty-five; he did penance for a superabundance of notes by
carrying music, in his uncompromising and spare late pieces,
to the brink of silence.
   To be sure, the excess of worship bestowed on him by
blind admirers, and the biographical semi-fiction fabricated
by his mistress Carolyne Sayn-Wittgenstein in conjunction
with Lina Ramann, was bound to provoke criticism. Here
Liszt must take some of the blame. At the end of a
questionnaire submitted to him by Miss Ramann before she
completed the first volume of her biography, Liszt, to her
bewilderment, volunteered the advice: 'Don't get too entangled in details. My biography has to be made up rather than
made out.' ('Meine Biographie ist weit mehr zu erfinden als
nachzuschreiben.') Meanwhile, even his renunciation of
public concerts (except for charity) and his taking minor
orders have been turned into acts of Lisztian self-promotion.
To steer clear of the devotional figure on the one side, and
the vulgarian of films and gossip magazines on the other, one
needs precise information, and good will. The most urgent
requirement, however, is that of musical fairness. A musical

charter of human rights, if there were such a concept, would grant any composer the basic privilege of being judged by his finest works, and their worthiest performances. Whether this Liszt year has brought us any nearer to such an ideal state of affairs remains the question.

*(1986)*

# Liszt's 'Années de pèlerinage' I and II

Next to the B minor Sonata, Liszt's *Années de pèlerinage* seem to me one of his finest achievements. The first two *Années* combine a youthful directness – the material for most of the pieces comes from his late twenties – with the advanced clarity and control of the Weimar period, while the Third Year offers generous examples of Liszt's late style before it shrank into fragmentary, and enigmatic, brevity.

The B minor Sonata should convert all those who have chosen to see Liszt mainly as an assimilator of styles and tunes not his own, and as a composer who could never truly finish a piece. The *Années de pèlerinage*, on the other hand, draw for their inspiration on a reservoir of diverse impressions – nature and musical folklore, art and religion, craving for freedom; above all, on poetry and literature.

Arriving at the final version was not always easy. Liszt, the improviser, composed at an awesome speed that hardly allowed time for reflection. The sometimes chaotic and overwritten music of his virtuoso years needed to be organized and purified. It became Liszt's habit to amend at least some details of his earlier works when he returned to them later on, unless he preferred to recompose whole sections. (In the case of the 'Chapelle de Guillaume Tell', barely a faint memory of one theme has survived.) Invariably, it is the poetic idea of each piece that continues to fire Liszt's musical imagination. It would be a mistake to assume that the greater transparency and fluency of the later versions involves a sacrifice of such pianistic obstacles as are musically relevant; rather, monstrosities are purged, or reduced to human scale.

Of the nine pieces that make up the Swiss Year, two ('Au lac de Wallenstadt' and 'Eglogue') have remained virtually untouched. A third one, 'Orage', was composed at a later date (1855). Of the rest, Liszt's Weimar versions are clearly superior, or at least, as in 'Pastorale' and 'Le mal du pays', equally successful. Only in the opening of 'Les cloches de Genève' has Liszt's slimming resulted in anaemia; the piano writing of the early draft is so much more seductive that I have decided to retain it, along with some details from the original 'Vallée d'Obermann'.

The early versions of the Swiss Year had been published in Liszt's *Album d'un voyageur*. To be a wanderer and pilgrim, not belonging anywhere, and looking for a place to belong, was a central concept of Romanticism. George Sand's *Lettres d'un voyageur*, Byron's *Childe Harold's Pilgrimage* and Schubert's various 'Wanderers' must have contributed to Liszt's frame of mind, as did E.P. de Sénancour's *Obermann*, in whose footsteps Liszt and Marie d'Agoult roamed through Switzerland, just as their Italian route followed that of Goethe, Chateaubriand and Madame de Staël in the foot-steps of Montesquieu. The writers who inspired Liszt's Swiss Year shared a disdain for convention while oscillating between ecstatic lyricism and a sceptical (Sénancour) or cynical (Byron) outlook on life.

Of Beethoven's developmental approach to composition which permeates Liszt's B minor Sonata, the *Années de pèlerinage* show no trace; the first two 'Years' are much closer to Berlioz and Franco-Italian opera[1] than to the Austro-German masters. What united most Romantics, however, was the disavowal of predictable forms on one side and the striving for an ultimate simplicity on the other.

## Première année: Suisse

The First Year of Pilgrimage (Switzerland) deals with nature in a twofold sense: as nature around us, and as the nature within. Liszt's own nature was full of compassion; his charitable disposition had a direct bearing on his revolution-

---

[1] Rossini's *Guillaume Tell* had been first performed in Paris in 1829.

ary sympathies. In 'Lyon', a piece later discarded, Liszt commemorates the uprising of textile workers. Visiting the 'Chapelle de Guillaume Tell', he is reminded of the Swiss struggle for liberation. In the central section the signals of revolt reverberate through the mountainside until 'freedom' is achieved. Three different kinds of dotted rhythm make for diversity within the unity. (Appropriately, Schiller's well-known line 'Einer für Alle, Alle für Einen' – 'One for all, all for one' – is the motto.) Musically, the piece is close to Bellini, whom Liszt had transferred to the piano in some of his grandest paraphrases.

Byron's lines which preface 'Au lac de Wallenstadt' contrast the stillness of the lake with the 'wild world'. Should one not 'forsake Earth's troubled waters for a purer spring'? The beginning of the piece rivals Schubert's ability to distil the essence of a song in an initial figure; here it is the movement of the oars, the gliding over the lake and the melancholy of twilight that are established before a yodelling melody comes in. In the first of his *Moments musicaux*, Schubert had provided a mountain tune as well as its musical mountain range. Liszt's *chant montagnard* is, on its later appearances, embellished with echoes and spiky contours. The elegance of 'Au lac de Wallenstadt' is Mendelssohnian, with the added bonus of *plein air* painting. As in 'Pastorale' and 'Eglogue', Liszt demonstrates the high art of being natural, and makes it hard to decide whether such delicious simplicity should be taken as the reverse of romantic *raffinement* or, rather, as its very peak.

In contrast to his impressionist descendants, Liszt experienced nature through the eyes of literature. 'Pastorale' may be an exception: in it, without any accompanying words, an ancient alphorn melody is presented in a straightforward manner. The only whiff of artifice is the alternation of veiled and distinct areas of sound.

After these two vignettes of rural life, two splendid poetic études follow. 'Au bord d'une source' (Allegretto grazioso, dolce tranquillo) creates the illusion of a shimmering multitude of drops by means of delicately clashing or suspended seconds. Again, the printed words give the player valuable information: Schiller tells him that the 'games of young nature' begin in 'murmuring coolness' – which may prevent him from turning the piece into a fountain of perfume.

In relation to 'Orage', some lines by Byron speculate on the nature of tempests. 'Are ye like those within the human breast? Or do ye find, at length, like eagles, some high nest?' There is certainly no 'high nest' for the storm unleashed here in torrential octaves; it remains an elemental uproar in the blackest C minor.

In 'Vallée d'Obermann', a superb fantasy on the first three notes of its opening theme, the gates of the human breast are again wide open, yet this is less a passionate symbol of surrounding nature than a vehicle for grandiose introspection and personal confession. Thanks to Sainte-Beuve's recommendation, Sénancour's *Obermann* became a favourite of a whole generation of French Romantics. Liszt called it 'the monochord of the relentless solitude of human pain', but also 'the book that soothes my sufferings'. For Obermann, the intellectual drop-out and radical sceptic, every cause is hidden, every purpose deceptive, and nature remains impenetrable. The opening of 'Vallée d'Obermann' paints a musical picture of solitary despair. As it turns into major keys, however, the piece adopts Sénancour's belief that the only dependable truth is in one's own feelings: 'to feel, to exist – only to be consumed by irresistible desire, to become intoxicated by the spell of an unreal world, and finally to perish in its beguiling deception'.

In utmost contrast, 'Eglogue' is all lightness and graceful perfection. Byron describes the morning, 'with cheek all bloom, laughing the clouds away with playful scorn'. The title of the piece refers to Virgil who, in his bucolic poetry, had erected a vision of an Arcadia that is removed from reality, an elevated land of blessed being into which Liszt introduces us with the help of a Swiss shepherd song.

Another long quotation from *Obermann* muses on the romantic effects of nature in the unspoilt countryside: they are 'the sounds of a primeval language not intelligible to all people'. In a footnote, Liszt himself calls such 'hidden sanctuaries' 'the last refuge of a free and simple mind'.

'Le mal du pays' is based on a *ranz-des-vaches* (herdsman's melody) from the Appenzell that had been mentioned as early as 1710 in an essay on the impact of homesickness. This impact, according to Rousseau, was so devastating that the playing of *ranz-des-vaches* among Swiss mercenaries had been forbidden on pain of death. While the first version of 'Le mal du pays' treats its rhapsodic alphorn tune (and some other Swiss melodies) without comment, as it were, the second version adds the psychological connotations of homesickness: within the E minor melancholy, brief episodes in major keys open up like visions of an unattainable paradise. 'Happiness is where you are not' – this statement of a fundamental Romantic experience had been composed by Schubert in his song 'Der Wanderer'.[1]

The last piece of the Swiss Year, 'Les cloches de Genève', makes do, in its final version, without any dedication or motto. It moves away from the literary sphere, and into a private one – a song of love in the expansive style of Liszt's 'Cantique d'amour' or 'Bénédiction'. Only the definitive version contains this cantilena: by then, the Princess Sayn-Wittgenstein had supplanted Marie d'Agoult (and the new-born Blandine to whom the first version was dedicated) as the mistress of Liszt's emotions. The introduction of the piece projects the sounds of distant nocturnal bells, dream-like and beguiling. According to Liszt, the player should surprise himself, and play the beginning as if 'unprepared'.

## *Deuxième année: Italie*

The Second Year (Italy) of the *Années* focuses on works of art and literature. 'Sposalizio' (after Raphael's *Betrothal of the*

---

[1] In a less romantic mood, Liszt called the same statement 'la maxime du bonheur conjugal', according to his daughter Cosima (*Franz Liszt, ein Gedenkblatt von seiner Tochter*, Bruckmann, 1911).

*Virgin* in Milan) manages to employ highly sophisticated harmony in order to create an aura of elated innocence. Its initial melodic figure – pentatonic, undulating, and seemingly improvised – turns out to be of greater significance than the cantabile themes; increasingly, it casts an exotic spell over the piece that looks forward to Debussy.

'Il penseroso' stunningly anticipates Wagnerian harmony. It refers to a sculpture and a poem by Michelangelo whose quatrain 'The Speech of Night' serves as a clue to the music: 'I am grateful to be asleep, and more grateful to be made of stone, as long as injustice and shame remain on earth. I count it a blessing not to see or feel; so do not wake me – speak softly!' The sculpture is a statue on the tomb of Lorenzo de' Medici in Florence. Liszt wanted this piece, in an augmented orchestral version, to be performed at his own funeral.

'Canzonetta del Salvator Rosa', a carefree marching song, is a later addition to the set. Its allusions seem threefold: to Salvator Rosa the adventurer, who wrote its words ('While I often change my place of being, the fire of my love remains unchanged'); to Salvator Rosa the baroque painter, whose self-portrait in the National Gallery in London reveals a remarkable physical likeness to Liszt himself; and, unwittingly, to Giovanni Bononcini who wrote the tune. (This is the only arrangement of somebody else's music within the set.)

The three Petrarch Sonnets are very free transcriptions of songs Liszt wrote before 1839. Both the early piano versions and the songs were extensively reworked in the Weimar years. In his 'Sonetto 47' Petrarch blesses the hour when Laura cast her first glance upon him, in spite of the longing, the pain, the tears and the 'resonance of sighs' that it has brought in its wake. 'Sonetto 104' evokes the ambivalence of love. The poem tells of its freezing glow, its seeing blindness and its weeping laughter. 'While I hate myself, I ardently love others.' Liszt's treatment of this array of oxymorons is intensely powerful, and on an almost constant level of *forte*; only the epilogue gives in to resignation – 'This is what you, my mistress, have done to me.'

'Sonetto 123' lifts us into an unearthly state: Laura is seen as an angel. Her tears are capable of softening stones and stopping rivers. Of such tenderness are her words that even the heavens hold their breath, and no leaf dares move. The final expiring of the piece seems to conclude all conclusions, and brings the sequence of the first six pieces to a close.

'Après une lecture du Dante' has adopted the title of a poem by Victor Hugo that begins with the line 'The poet who paints Hell paints his own life'. The relation between the A flat of the preceding 'Sonetto 123' and its own key of D minor is that of a tritone: *diabolus in musica*. The opening theme of the Dante Fantasy is based on tritones as well; according to Liszt's pupil Stradal, it does *not* represent the inscription above Dante's gate of Hell, but should be understood as a call to the spirits of the damned to rise – 'Step out, shadows, from the realm of misery and distress!' The chromatic theme (Presto agitato assai) then suggests the approach and wailing of the damned – their contours blurred by Liszt's direction to maintain a continuous five-bar pedal – while the first appearance of the chorale (F sharp major, *fff*, double octaves) is a portrait of Lucifer.

After the return of the rousing tritones, the music depicts the Francesca da Rimini episode: 'Nessun maggior dolore, che ricordarsi del tempo felice nella miseria' ('There is no greater sorrow than to remember happy times while in misery'). Later on, in Stradal's view, the damned mock, split up and trivialize their themes of grief. The piece is as near to Berlioz as anything Liszt ever wrote, yet strikingly original. It is rightly subtitled 'Fantasia quasi sonata' and not, as in Beethoven's Op. 27, 'Sonata quasi una fantasia'. The concept of the fantasy remains variable; while relating to the familiar forms, it makes free use of them, calls them into question, tears them apart, or amalgamates several at once. Not until the B minor Sonata did Liszt compose a large-scale work in which the psychological cohesion is matched by the cohesion of musical structure.

*(1985)*

# Liszt's B minor Sonata

If, as I believe, the B minor Sonata represents the exception among Liszt's works, what is the rule? For me, Liszt is a master of the shorter format, the creator of the religiously inspired piano piece, the magical transformer and unchallenged orchestrator of piano sound, the generous musical poet, visionary and revolutionary. Pieces the size of 'Vallée d'Obermann', 'Funérailles' or the Variations on Bach's 'Weinen, Klagen, Sorgen, Zagen' show his command of an often innovatory idiom. His musical imagination is nourished by a large variety of intellectual and emotional food; literature and the arts, religion and nature, personalities and ideas, the political struggle for freedom and an awareness of death all contribute to it. The B minor Sonata, on the other hand, the most original, powerful and intelligent sonata composed after Beethoven and Schubert, is a work of absolute music, and it exemplifies total control of large form. Its blend of deliberation and white heat, unique in Liszt's output, remains all the more astonishing as it was achieved in the face of a most demanding task: a one-movement sonata of half an hour's duration.

## Themes, Characters

What, in comparison with Liszt's 'Faust' Symphony, becomes immediately evident is that none of the themes is a disappointment. Six strongly individual characters are introduced − I shall call them themes, and ignore the controversial aspects of this term. The first impression produced by these themes, their initial character, remains, despite all later metamorphosis, the main source of information for the listener who does not want to lose his bearings.

 The first three themes are presented one after the other.

173

They could be called an introductory group. (Whether one perceives the Sonata to contain four, five or six themes depends on one's view of this group; one could also subdivide it into two, separating the passive Lento theme from the two active Allegro characters.)

The *First Theme* (Lento, sotto voce, quasi G minor, bars 1–7) relates sound to silence. Syncopations are preceded by 'accented' rests. Musically, the theme is representative not of speech or singing, but of thinking. Interspersed between short, muted blows on G – quasi timpani plus pizzicato – one hears two descending scales, the Phrygian and the gypsy scale. Questions are posed, doubts arise. Harmonic expectations, if any, point towards C minor.

I have come across two commercial recordings of the Sonata that omit the first bar. The sound engineers, apparently assuming that the pianist had not seriously started, edited it away. Little did they know that a good sonata exposes its basic material at once. Thus the repeated notes of this beginning are among the motifs that are important to the whole work. (Each of the themes takes off from, or is introduced by, repeated notes.) Other motifs to remember are the intervals of the seventh and the second, as well as the opening rhythm.

In the *Second Theme* (Allegro energico, B minor, bars 8–13) an actor makes his grand entrance on stage. His attitude is a mixture of defiance, despair and contempt. May I call him Faust? Not before the angry octave triplets in bar 10 do we realize that B minor may be the basic key.

The *Third Theme* (Marcato, bars 14–18) follows suit. It counters Faust's questions with its own. The character, instigating subversion, is Mephistophelean. Faust and Mephisto join, fifteen bars later, to produce what could be called a symphonic main idea (sempre forte ed agitato). With the initial group the presentation of motivic material comes to an end. All remaining themes now belong to major keys.

The *Fourth Theme* (Grandioso, D major, bars 105–113) is derived from the first in rhythm and melodic substance. It is preceded by a transition on a pedal point that is as gripping as anything the work has to offer. The word 'grandioso' is appropriately chosen for a theme that carries the conviction of omnipotence.[1]

The *Fifth Theme* (Cantando espressivo, D major, bars 153–170) sets out as a lyrical variant of the third: Mephisto turned into a vision of Gretchen – if, for the sake of enlivening the terminology and simplifying description, one agrees to accept such verbal crutches in a work that makes do without them. Nine bars later we discover Faust to be under Gretchen's spell; there is no doubt about it that we experience the events of this work from his point of view. The first eight bars of the theme are clearly based, in its bass line, on Theme 1 (seventh and descending scale).

The *Sixth Theme* (Andante sostenuto, F sharp major, bars 331–346) is, musically, less a matter of character than of idea. To stay with Goethe, I am reminded of 'the eternal feminine that transports us to higher spheres'. Although the Sixth Theme appears independent, it does relate to previous themes. Its beginning paraphrases the climax of the Grandioso theme, projected into a transparent distance. In its later course, the First Theme (tone repetition and descending minor scale) is lovingly enriched by the ascending major

---

[1] I cannot reconcile myself to recent religious interpretations of the Sonata. Surely any religious view of the work must stand or fall by assessment of the so-called 'Cross motif'. If its use in the amorous B major tune of the E flat major Concerto, or the grotesquely exuberant march from the same work with its cymbal crash, marks these themes as religious, then all music might well be called religious, in the manner in which all art was deemed political not too long ago. The Grandioso theme of the Sonata is, to me, ruled out as a theme of religious character by the imperious gesture of its ending, which suggests, to a psychologically inclined listener, megalomania rather than omnipotence.

Having played a good number of Liszt's religious pieces, I have found them to be distinguished by a specific poetry, a devotional aura, rather than by intervals of a motif the use of which is as little confined to the religious sphere as Liszt's religious music can be defined by it. For me, the Faust-Mephisto-Gretchen constellation does better justice to the Sonata as I understand it. However, it remains a working hypothesis, and my personal luxury. The B minor Sonata does not need a programme.

seventh. The use of the seventh in this sonata would deserve an essay of its own; nothing may be more indicative of the work than the expressive quality of this interval.

A multitude of emotions, contrasts, colour and texture is mobilized to justify the dimensions of the piece. Within its vast area of tension, the unity of its motivic material seems to me of more than little importance. What I am hinting at is not the transformation of themes, rather typical of Liszt, which leaves them clearly distinguishable while their character and atmosphere change. It is Beethoven's much more subtle technique of relating all themes and movements to one another through common motivic denominators that, in this work, is also applied by Liszt.

Another procedure inherited from Beethoven is the technique of 'foreshortening'. If Liszt, as impatient critics have claimed, chose in this sonata to 'say everything twice', he used this pattern to clarify the structure. Where the pattern is broken, usually a foreshortening process has come to an end. The possibilities of saying things twice are diverse enough; they comprise variants (First Theme), sequences (Second and Third Themes), varied (Fifth Theme) or elaborated sequences (Sixth Theme), and identical repeats ('symphonic main idea').

## Form, Structure

Liszt's amalgamation of first-movement form and the movements of a sonata within one structure must have been inspired by the finale of Beethoven's Ninth Symphony and Schubert's 'Wanderer' Fantasy, both of which Liszt knew intimately. In the B minor Sonata, the F sharp Andante stands for the slow movement, while the fugato has some features of a scherzo, though not the usual one in 3/4 or 3/8; its short staccato and rhythmic layout are reminiscent of the unorthodox 'scherzo' in Beethoven's Sonata Op. 31 No. 3.

A brief outline of the B minor Sonata may be content to show that a fiercely modulating exposition is based, as much as necessary, on the keys of B minor and D major; that the F sharp major Andante occupies the space of the development; and that, depending on catholicism of taste, the fugato, or else the return of the 'symphonic main idea', indicates the beginning of the recapitulation. In its course, all the themes that previously did not have a chance to appear in the basic tonality are permitted to do so. Is it really as simple as that? Let me try to investigate some of the events of the work in greater detail.

(*a*) *Exposition. First Development. First False Recapitulation.* There are plenty of development sections in this sonata. The themes themselves, instead of being, in Liszt's well-known style, merely clad in different garments or presented in a different light, are given to all manner of developments and combinations. The exposition of the Fifth Theme is followed by a modulating section that, in spite of lacking a clearly defined onset, could well be mistaken for the main development: it does lead back into the First Theme in such a grand way that we may ask ourselves whether the recapitulation has started at bar 277. We expect the Second Theme to reappear in B minor, confirming recapitulation and basic key. Instead, this theme is chiselled into the piano in the 'wrong' key of F minor (deciso, bar 286). Our harmonic expectations have been surpassed. We find ourselves not in the recapitulation but in a

(*b*) *Recitativo* section, rugged and punctuated by rests, that starts with C sharp minor chords (*fff* pesante, bar 297). The opening of the Fourth (Grandioso) Theme now sounds merciless and monumental: it brings the propulsive drive of the exposition to a halt. Faust reacts in a free variant of the retrograde. His argument with fate should never be allowed to degenerate into hysterical or whimpering self-pity. Liszt's *forte* markings, indicated in both hands, are all too often ignored. During a long, Mephisthophelean pedal point on B the fire of Faust's defiance burns down. The whole section ends on the dominant of E minor.

(*c*) *'Slow Movement' (Andante): Middle Section with Second Development.* Again, Liszt surpasses our harmonic expecta-

tions. The surprise of F sharp major and a new, Sixth Theme
strikes us like a vision of a better world. The air is pure:
during the exposition the key of F sharp had been left out.
After a sustained spell of rapture that includes the Fifth
(Gretchen) Theme in its entirety, the actual development
takes up the declamatory gesture of the recitativo section. Its
drama, however, is now channelled into symphonic continuity. The magnificent climax it leads to, thematically identical
with the beginning of the middle section (Sixth Theme), is
dynamically its opposite: the 'eternal feminine' overwhelms
us with all-embracing power. It is one of the most moving
moments of the work, and one of the most demanding for
the player, when triumph suddenly turns into sweetness.
Gradually tension gives way to calm; the key of F sharp major
is never left. During thirty-eight bars, time stops. The
audience forgets to breathe – or so the pianist hopes. The
First Theme appears in F sharp, bringing the middle section
to a close and, at the same time, leading into the fugato.
Having returned to the origin of the piece, we expect to
renew our acquaintance with Faust and Mephisto.

(*d*) *Fugato; simultaneously Second False Recapitulation, Third
Development and 'Scherzo'*. I do not know what to admire most:
the introduction of a fugato at this point; the anticipations it
fulfils or ironically disappoints; how three-part writing
gradually grows back into 'symphonic' texture; the Mozar-
tian effortlessness of its polyphony; the originality that sets
this fugato apart from baroque stereotypes that held sway
well into the nineteenth century; or its manifold connotations that recall a picture puzzle.

Faust and Mephisto reappear; the fugato theme makes
room for both of them. The constellation of the Sonata's very
beginning has once more materialized, and everything bodes
well for the recapitulation. But why are Faust and Mephisto
leaping around on tiptoe? Why do they talk in a sarcastic
whisper? The 'spirit of negation' seems to have taken hold of
both of them; but is there, musically speaking, an object of
negation? It is, so we begin to realize, the basic key of B
minor in which the recapitulation, according to classical

rules, should have started. Actually, the fugato proves to be in the 'wrong' key of B flat minor, one semitone too low.

What is the purpose of this dislocation of a section that could also be called the Third Development, and a contrasting section with scherzo character? The clue is in the long, transfixed dwelling on F sharp that precedes it, and the tonal solidity of the recapitulation that follows. The fugato, harmonically scintillating and extraterritorial, separates both stable sections and postpones the takeover of the basic key.

(*e*) *Recapitulation and Epilogue*. It is only where the Second and Third Themes are fused together (bar 533) that we reach the key of B minor; we shall not seriously move away from it again. For the rest of the piece, light (B major) and darkness (B minor) fight against one another, with the light eventually triumphant. Compared with the exposition, the recapitulation is considerably more terse as a result of the limited harmonic scope. Not only the Fourth and Fifth Themes, but also both false recapitulations are brought home into the basic key (the second one first, from bar 569 on, then the first from bar 673). The domination of B major is frantically underlined by a tornado of rapid octaves and vibrating chord repetitions – an extrovert climax that hardly challenges the true, inner climax of the work in the central section of the Sonata.

Enthusiasm switches, after an extensive silence, to sudden introspection: the coda brings back the quiet Sixth Theme in the key of B major. Peace is found. A few bars before the end, the First Theme makes a final appearance, at last in the home key. With the last bass note, all tension is resolved.

We cannot thank Liszt enough for deciding against a projected fortissimo ending. The seven lines that took its place have enriched the Sonata beyond measure. In toto, this work is beautifully finished. Neither *ossias* nor suggestions for cuts betray improvisatory haste. The performer should, wisely, avoid treating the piece as a bizarre and feverish dream. One thing has to lead inevitably into the next. Each note has its place. The markings, similar to those of later Beethoven or Brahms, indicate the essential with admirable clarity.

Liszt's B minor Sonata was finished on 2 February 1853. It is dedicated to Schumann in return for Schumann's dedication of his C major Fantasy to Liszt. In 1854, when the Sonata appeared in print, Schumann had retired from the world into an asylum. Neither his wife Clara nor her friend Brahms, for whom Liszt had played the Sonata in Weimar, was able to appreciate it. Wagner was the only one to accept it with joy. As late as 1857, Hans von Bülow premièred the piece in Berlin.

*(1981)*

# Liszt's Bitterness of Heart

It was left to our time to discover Liszt's late piano pieces. They establish the Mephistophelean abbé as a founding father of the music of our century, a fact some experts had noticed before. But these works were considered suitable for reading, not for performance. Only recently, almost a hundred years after they were written, have they emerged as music that can be played and conveyed to a listening public.

It is not, however, from the nineteenth-century concert stage, from the pomp and intoxication of virtuosity, that these works grow. They do not seek to be persuasive; they hardly even seek to convince. In Liszt's own words, 'exuberance of heart' gave way to 'bitterness of heart', a bitterness that had various sources: the death of Liszt's children Daniel and Blandine, his inability to marry Carolyne Sayn-Wittgenstein, the disappointment in his friendships with Wagner and Bülow, and the lack of appreciation of his works. 'Infirmary music' was his own term for much of what he then composed. He apparently let Hungarian friends believe that he wrote the *Csárdás macabre* to irk his powerful adversary, the Viennese critic Eduard Hanslick.

This piano piece, unpublished until the 1950s, is one in the series of *danses macabres* and Mephistophelean waltzes, of elegies and threnodies, memorials and troubled inspirations which afflicted Liszt in his last fifteen years. The macabre element is no longer picturesquely theatrical, as in *Totentanz*; neither is it the motive that triggers revolutionary pathos, as in *Funérailles*. 'Is it permissible to write something like that, or to listen to it?' asked Liszt's pupil Göllerich when he saw *Csárdás*. His question sounds like an echo of what Liszt himself had written thirty years earlier about Chopin's *Polonaise fantaisie*; it shows how greatly Liszt had changed.

What Wagner's musical friendship amounted to at this

181

time is revealed in a comment on Liszt's late works. Wagner considered them the 'picture of a world in decline', with 'decadent Paris', which he so much hated, as its centre. The remark, though meant contemptuously, contains a grain of truth. Most of Liszt's late piano pieces are indeed documents of two declines, that of tonality and that of human personality in old age.

Liszt was probably the first composer to experience the dissolution of tonality in his work, and to free himself from its domination. In his late piano music he avoids traditional cadences. He hardly ever modulates; instead, he puts keys or harmonies side by side, gliding from one to another chromatically, modally, or by means of the gypsy scale. The assurance with which this happens caused Busoni to remark that 'the harmony of a revolutionary lies in the steady hand of a sovereign'. When impressions of tonality in the customary sense are conveyed, their effect is one of wistful or ironic reminiscences of the past, or of excursions into a sphere of childlike feeling (as in the *Christmas Tree* suite dedicated to Liszt's granddaughter Daniela). Frequently, as in *Aux cyprès de la Villa d'Este I*, *Unstern* or *Schlaflos, Frage und Antwort*, a dissonant and obsessive first section is answered by a consonant section – usually in a church mode – which could be taken as a gesture of humility, as an appeasement hardly approaching consolation, a desire to be protected by the shelter of a convention that has become an enigma, and no longer offers safety or hope.

The classic-romantic forms drew their meaning from the functional harmony of major and minor; once their tonal foundation was shattered, they became meaningless. Instead of symmetry, development and recapitulation, Liszt now used the simple confrontation of extreme contrasts or the coexistence of two keys: F major and D major in *Csárdás macabre*, F minor and B major in *Unstern*. Other pieces are not afraid to present the arbitrary or fragmentary, to become torpid, to fade away, to forget where they started when they stop. In this they reflect the symptoms of ageing. We must be careful to distinguish between a shrinkage of elements of the personality in old age, and a decline of creative power (of which Liszt was rather unjustly accused). No composer stayed younger to the very end in his urge and ability to create something new. 'Accidental form', which brought an element of insecurity to many of his earlier works, now comes into its own. It finds suitable material: the dread of senility, as well as displaced harmony – displaced largely by the use of the gypsy scale (originally Indian) and its derivatives. The old man himself is displaced; not even Hungary wants to listen to his music, while he strays between Weimar, Pest and Rome.

What is new in Liszt's late piano pieces is presented without mitigation, spotlit by radical simplicity. The melody dispenses with traditional ideas of cantabile. Lonely unison effects are explored. Tone colour remains an important source of the music's impact, but now it is predominantly the dark and the glaring, the ashen and the ethereal that move or unsettle us. The rhythm is obsessive, harassing, oppressive, or it tries to dissolve into the air. Even the smallest piece has breadth; there are hardly any miniatures of the order of Schumann's *Papillons* or *Kinderszenen*, or Schoenberg's Op. 19.

It seems as if the shrinking of the ageing personality has left room for the impersonal, for an archaic force. Liszt's former lavishness, at the time artistically legitimate, has disappeared. There is an unexpected link with late Schubert. In his virtuoso days, Liszt overwhelmed the public, even that of Vienna, with his transcriptions of Schubert's songs; but in them he often treated Schubert badly, transposing him to the level of his own rhetorical exuberance. As an old composer, Liszt approaches the original Schubert at his most depressive. Songs like 'Der Doppelgänger', 'Der Leiermann' or 'Die Stadt' lead in a direct line to pieces like *Unstern* and *Mosonyi*. They have in common the union of brevity and monumentality, the declamatory and the pithy, monotony and refinement.

To me, many of Liszt's late pieces seem to anticipate a discovery that took place in the visual arts at the turn of the century: that of the 'primitive' or 'barbaric', as seen for example in Gauguin's Tahiti, in masks from Africa and Oceania, or in early Romanesque sculpture. (Goethe, the paragon of civilized man, spoke in 1805 of an 'irresistible propensity for the absurd which causes the hereditary savagery of grimace-loving primitives to resurface in the most respectable world, contrary to all culture'.) But there are distinctions: where the Fauves drew their inspiration from 'primitive' tribal art, or Picasso from Pyrenean wood sculpture, Liszt drew his grimacing visions from himself. There were, to be sure, additional contributions from sources as disparate as the gypsies, the younger Russian composers, and Gregorian chant; but the most important impulse came from the musical situation of the time – from the dissolution of tonality and the forms depending on it. The title of one of his last pieces indicates that Liszt was aware of what he was doing: in the *Bagatelle without Tonality* even passing attachments to a key are avoided. Almost independent of Wagner's *Tristan* chromaticism, and more consistently than any of his contemporaries, Liszt ushers in the music of the twentieth century.

What should interest us most in these pieces, however, is not what they anticipate or prepare the ground for, but what they are. They hardly need excuses – not even for being experiments; that word can be much more fittingly applied to early works like *Malédiction* or the piano piece *Harmonies poétiques et religieuses*. The unity of Liszt's late style, and the diversity within that unity, can be comprehended only by listening to a whole set of these pieces, one after another – and in performances that do not impose on them a concept of paralysing slowness and pallor. Liszt's entire range of pianistic refinement, acquired over long years of experience, has a part to play even in the most awkward sounds this music makes. An enormous stock of nuances should be felt to be available in the background, even when they seem to remain unused.

Two of Liszt's late pieces are exceptions, in that they soon gained a place in the standard repertory. If they are not among the most typical (and that is why they were accepted), they are certainly among the most beautiful. The first *Valse oubliée*, a concise piece characterized by a supremely elegant and slightly diabolical air of seduction, helps to explain why Liszt attracted the favours of the fair sex up to the very end. The waltz anticipates Skriabin by decades, just as *Les jeux d'eau à la Villa d'Este*, 'the model for all musical fountains that have flowed ever since' (Busoni), gives a foretaste of impressionism. Unlike these later fountains, their earlier model is also, and above all, religious music. Most of the other pieces in the third volume of *Années de pèlerinage* are likewise religious in character, in contrast to those of the earlier *Années*, which depict nature or evoke works of literature and art. In *Aux cyprès de la Villa d'Este I* the melancholy and menace emanating from the huge shapes of cypresses gives way to Christian consolation in unhackneyed chromaticism. (After 1864, Liszt used to live in an apartment at the Villa d'Este when he stayed in Rome.)

*Sunt lacrymae rerum* is another threnody, but one with a Hungarian flavour. The words of the title, taken from Book I of Virgil's *Aeneid*, refer to the fall of Troy; Liszt, however, used them as an allusion to the failure of the Hungarian revolution of 1848–9. But there is another, more personal allusion. In 1872, the year the piece was written, Liszt visited Bayreuth for the first time. There he accused Wagner and Cosima of having ruined the life of his outstanding pupil, Hans von Bülow, whose marriage to Liszt's daughter had broken up because of Wagner. Not surprisingly, *Sunt lacrymae rerum* is dedicated to Bülow; it contains some of the blackest sounds ever produced in the bass register of a concert grand.

*(1980)*

# Busoni's 'Doktor Faust'

Busoni's involvement with opera was linked to his concept of a 'Junge Klassizität'. It was not the turning back to older forms, or the ironic comment on past styles, of neoclassicism that Busoni had in mind; his strangely Utopian notion envisaged a music removed from the constraints of purpose, style, form and functional harmony. What 'Junge Klassizität' shares with classicism is a mistrust of an emotional intensity that goes overboard, of flamboyant gestures, and of a sensuality or 'sexuality' that in music, though by no means in life, Busoni thought ridiculous and untruthful. Love duets, including that of Verdi's *Otello*, made him furious: there is nothing more appalling, he notes, than a little man and a large lady pouring gushing melodies over one another while holding hands.

Musically, Busoni hoped for an end to 'thematic' or 'motivic' composition, called for the primacy of melody in all voices (linear polyphony) and helped, along with Schoenberg, to emancipate dissonance. To him, dissonance rather than the triad represented 'nature'. (With all their differences in musical outlook, Busoni patiently continued to support Schoenberg, whose existence in Berlin rested largely on his backing. Alas, Schoenberg declined to complete *Doktor Faust* after Busoni's death, but accepted the offer to succeed him as composition teacher at the Prussian Academy.)

Busoni's ideas reacted against the inflated rhetoric and the sentimental pathos of late romanticism, Italian verismo, and expressionism. (Busoni conceded that there is an expressionist in every composer, but rejected any claims of supremacy of one style over another.) He steered clear of kitsch in a musical period that, even in some of its most gifted exponents, was prone to kitsch in unprecedented measure. To an audience used to overheated and over-stimulated music, Busoni's self-control must have appeared almost glacial. In music, he explains, feeling has to be applied

186

grandly and economically. It should not be overly concerned with detail, and wasted on the short span (this is what, according to Busoni, the layman, the mediocre artist and, one may be tempted to add, some American critics, conceive feeling to be). Feeling needs to be linked to taste and style. The popular concept of feeling ignores taste: the result is sentimentality, and over-projection. To feeling that demonstrates itself in 'spontaneous' gestures, Busoni prefers feeling 'that acts quietly' and, most of all, feeling that is concealed.

Busoni's phobia about the trivial and ingratiating extended to the musically stereotyped. The 'typical' horn call, the melting string phrase, the chuckling bassoon, the instantly memorable tune belonged to a past that he greatly admired. As they became a matter of routine, one needed to avoid them. It was rather late in his development that Busoni, after writing his prophetic *Outline of a New Aesthetic of Music* (1907), imposed such strictures on himself, an austerity that, to him, opened up vast areas of freedom. If what Isaiah Berlin has termed 'moral charm' is applicable to musical aims, Busoni's offer proof of it.

Busoni believed that opera is the supreme form of musical expression because it permits, and demands, the combination of all musical means and forms. Opera, according to him, should not duplicate what happens on stage but illuminate what goes on in the mind, or soul, of the acting characters, unseen and unuttered. Not the thunderstorm but the reaction – or non-reaction – to it is what ought to be composed. In some special cases, the music may impress on the listener what happens outside his vision – behind the stage, so to speak – and ignore what can be clearly perceived. Singing texts on stage is a convention that has the effect of 'untruth'. Therefore, opera has to concentrate on the unbelievable and on what is unlikely to make sense of itself; the public should always be reminded that it is dealing with the fictional world of the jocular and/or fantastic that is unlike the seriousness and truthfulness of life.

The operatic subject Busoni sought – 'half religious' and elevating, yet entertaining – had to involve a quintessential and mysterious figure. After Ahasuerus and Dante, Leonardo was considered; as Antony Beaumont shows in his splendid book *Busoni the Composer*,[1] Busoni was able to identify with Leonardo in a variety of ways. He was discarded when Gabriele d'Annunzio, to our great good fortune, failed to provide a libretto. Don Juan – though Busoni saw him differently from da Ponte – was ruled out on account of Mozart's music, Goethe's *Faust* on account of Busoni's respect for Goethe's text. (In looking for a 'subject' that would not be complete without music, Busoni saw in *Faust II* a prime example of 'operatic drama'.) Finally, the medieval *Puppet Play of Doctor Faust* proved decisive: it promised, like the revered *Magic Flute*, a combination of the educational, the spectacular, the awesome and the amusing.

Busoni was a remarkable writer. His essays, and letters to his wife, testify to originality, erudition and stylistic grace. Busoni's libretto for *Doktor Faust* does not quite reach the level of his prose: it remains under the spell of Goethe's diction. Critics of the text of *Zauberflöte* or *Parsifal* – two scores Busoni greatly admired, and two libretti I find no less mystifying than his own – should have a field day. Busoni's Faust, at the end of his life, concentrates on an ultimate 'mysterious deed': he gives his own life to his dead child in order to live on as an 'eternal will'. By finally stepping out of the magic circle of beliefs, by leaving religious concepts, good and evil, God and the Devil, behind in Nietzschean fashion, Faust becomes free to draw his own magic circle, and create his own myth. How Faust is able to extract himself from the obligation to serve the forces of evil remains hard to comprehend. 'One good deed' seems an all too easy way out. Does Faust's lifting himself out of the morass – in the style of the German folk hero Münchhausen – by pulling his own hair, thereby undo his past crimes? In the end, the power of Mephistopheles that had frightened Faust out of his wits appears no less riddled with human frailty than that of the Queen of the Night, and Sarastro.

[1] Indiana University Press, 1985

It is, however, hardly the point of opera to be rational. Some of the mystifying events in Busoni's libretto may, to him, have had their private connotations (it should have amused him that Faust's pact with the Devil is sealed on an Easter Sunday – the day on which Busoni was born). Others, such as the two apparitions of Helen of Troy, Busoni's unattainable ideal of beauty and perfection, are frankly Utopian; the fusion of Utopianism and blasphemy in Helen's appearance on the Cross remains the most striking invention in Busoni's plot.

At his death, Busoni had not produced the music for the Helen of Troy episodes, or finished Faust's final monologue. To make performances possible, Philipp Jarnach, the most experienced of Busoni's pupils, was persuaded to complete the work. What he contributed, reluctantly and in uncomfortable haste, delighted the press of the day. To my ears it has always appeared diametrically opposed to Busoni's style, an intrusion of Wagner-cum-Leoncavallo into Busoni's rarefied air. (Of the composers influenced by Busoni, Varèse would have come closest to doing justice to the final scene. Kurt Weill, taking his cue from parts of the church intermezzo from *Doktor Faust*, created in due course his own refreshingly cynical brand of music theatre.)

Luckily, this obstacle to the appreciation of *Doktor Faust* has now been removed, thanks to Antony Beaumont's recent solution. His task was uniquely facilitated by Busoni's habit of using elements of his previous compositions where it suited him, or, indeed, of anticipating *Doktor Faust* in works like the 'Sonatina seconda' or the 'Berceuse élégiaque' that were to break fresh ground.

It would be unreasonable to expect from Mr Beaumont what Busoni himself did not accomplish. His concoction of Busoniana follows Busoni's own prescriptions with remarkable taste and skill. (Only months before his death, Busoni had outlined a musical design of the final scene in a sketch unknown to Jarnach at the time he made his completion.) Beaumont, unlike Jarnach, gives the full text of Faust's final monologue and has restored some lines that are crucial to the understanding, if that is the right word, of Faust's ultimate wisdom. In Beaumont's score, these lines of Nietzschean renunciation contain one instance of mistranslation. Beaumont's book gives a different, literal and accurate if not singable, text for 'Euch zum Trotze, Euch Allen, die ihr euch gut preist, die wir nennen böse' ('In defiance of you, of you all, who hold yourselves for good, whom we call evil'). Beaumont's score reads: 'Let me spite you, wreak my vengeance on all you good ones who in truth are evil', turning the goodies into baddies, and obscuring the issue that Faust rids himself of good and evil alike.

What is the sum of *Doktor Faust*'s parts? I think that, among operatic mystery plays, Busoni's *Faust* is musically superior to Pfitzner's *Palestrina* and Hindemith's *Mathis der Maler*, and invites comparison with Schoenberg's *Moses und Aron*. I find Busoni's score masterly, intensely personal, and admirably true to his aims. It seems uneroded, and incorruptible, by time. The tag of eclecticism that is habitually fastened around Busoni's neck fits neither his melodic invention nor his treatment of harmony; where he makes use of older forms he does so with innovative freedom; and his orchestration is never that of a pianist: it shows the most delicate and precise perception of the noblest tints of colour. My only doubts are about the end of the penultimate scene where Faust welcomes the last evening of his life with quite untypical bombast – avoidable if the drawn-out allargando is ignored – and the curiously thin opening of the final tableau. A large cut at the beginning of the final scene up to the second appearance of the nightwatchman would help the balance and cohesion of the whole work.

Scenically, there is enough for an inventive producer to build upon. (Busoni, in his libretto, intentionally left gaps to be filled in by the producer, and the public.) In David Pountney's highly imaginative presentation at the English National Opera,[1] the expressionist in Busoni was over-projected. Busoni himself would have been surprised, and

[1] 1986

thoroughly horrified, by some of Pountney's scenic coups, and by the reference to political actuality that was imposed on a timeless human problem. Pountney gave an amusing twist to the students' celebrating Faust's famulus Wagner as 'Rector Magnificus', and made the emergence of the naked boy from Faust's cloak a resoundingly moving experience. But he also turned Helen, who is supposed to appear in a classical landscape, into a harlot, omitted the required magic circles altogether, and remained tied to the all too dominating set by Stefanos Lazaridis that fitted neither the church scene, the Court of Parma nor the tavern, and evoked New York rather than Wittenberg. Busoni maintained that his libretto was free from philosophical intentions, and that the events of the final tableau sprang out of him in an 'entirely poetic' manner. Pountney, I feel, was guided too strongly by rationalizations, symbols and Jungian concepts. He claims, in the programme, that Busoni's Mephistopheles 'offers nothing truly devilish – only something human' (namely another part of Faust's personality), contradicting himself a little later in the same essay by stating that Mephistopheles grants Faust 'the superhuman and lethal ability to act out his thoughts' unrestrained. It is this superhuman faculty indeed that unleashes Faust's fate. All grumbles apart, Mr Pountney deserved his share of the credit for *Doktor Faust's* public success; not a few of those in the audience who were unaware of Busoni's intentions will have perceived his staging as meaningful and highly effective.

Musically, the ENO coped admirably with Busoni's extraordinary demands. Electronic amplification was used where, before its invention, Busoni seemed to call for it: the sound of the organ enveloped the listener as he had suggested. Antony Beaumont conducted the two performances that I heard. It was good to see somebody who writes so well about Busoni bringing his music so stylishly to life. Of all those involved in making this new version of *Doktor Faust* such a memorable occasion, he must take pride of place. Graham Clark, in every way the ideal exponent of Mephistopheles, mastered the 'impossible' tessitura triumphantly.

Thomas Allen's Faust was beautifully sung, though, at times, a little lacking in dynamic, and demonic, force. All gratitude to the ENO for finally presenting *Doktor Faust* on the London stage and making it an impressive event. The attendance, and rapture, at the Coliseum indicated that the time for Busoni may, after all, be coming.

*(1986)*

# Furtwängler

Wilhelm Furtwängler was the performing musician who, more than any other, provided me with the criteria for judging a performance. Not that I knew him personally; my career had just begun when Furtwängler's ended, and partnership with a great conductor of his age would have been no easy matter for a youngster anyway. But I had heard several of his concerts in Vienna, Salzburg and Lucerne, as well as a number of opera performances. These, and the records and tapes which since that time have kept me in touch with his conducting, have remained for me a most important source of reference as to what music-making is about.

The greatness of Furtwängler the conductor is, I think, best appreciated if one disregards Furtwängler the composer, the writer of essays, letters or diaries, the thinker (outside the purely musical sphere), the German patriot, as well as the person 'political' and 'non-political', childish and sophisticated, magnetic and absurdly irritable. Those who believe that the character of a musician has to be as elevating as the best of his music-making need read no further – a lot of great music will elude them. A young intellectual who, in conversation with Alban Berg, complained about Wagner's character was told by Berg: 'For you, as a non-musician, nothing could be easier than to condemn him.' Unlike Wagner, Furtwängler hardly qualifies as a villain. Yet I shall have to dissociate myself from some of his views, above all from his obsession with the overwhelming importance of German soul and spirit – that conviction about being chosen which, according to the eminent Zionist leader Nahum Goldmann, was, ironically, for some time a belief common to both Germans and Jews.[1] Then there is Furtwängler's belief, derived from

---

[1] 'Both peoples have been of importance in world history; but they have also felt,

193

Goethe, that 'the very great is never new', and his clinging to
tonal harmony, to the heritage of the classical and romantic
symphony, to popular intelligibility – even in the case of new
compositions – which in the end blinded him to the
achievements of twentieth-century music, and made him
overestimate his own. His definition of a composer as 'one
who can write his own folksong' suggests a dangerous affinity
with those who regard music as a controllable political tool.

Furtwängler considered himself primarily a composer,
and repeatedly spoke of the day when he would finally stop
conducting in order to do something truly worthwhile. But it
was not merely a matter of chance that this wish remained
unfulfilled. There was, of course, the fact that Furtwängler
had been successful as a conductor, whereas he remained
relatively unnoticed as a composer; but there must also have
been a critical instinct within him which told him that,
notwithstanding his belief in himself as a composer, conducting was where his powers of persuasion lay. All we need to
know about his compositions is that they helped him to look
at the works he conducted from a composer's point of view.

To those of us who do not seek access to music via the
detour of literature, philosophy or ideology, Furtwängler
remains indispensable. If Furtwängler had not existed, we
would have had to invent him. He was the conductor under
whose guidance a piece of music emerged as something
complete, alive in all its layers, every detail justified by its
breathing relevance to the whole. The prejudice among
some English-speaking critics that Furtwängler, carried away
by the musical moment, sacrificed unity and cohesion, is
more untrue of him than of anybody else. No conductor was,
in his greatest performances, freer yet less eccentric. No
other musician in my experience conveyed so strongly the
feeling that the fate of a piece (and of its performance) was
sealed with its first bar, and that its destiny would be fulfilled

---

and feel, their own importance to an unusual degree. Being excessively aware of
their importance, they take pride in it as well.' – Nahum Goldmann, 'Warum der
Nazi-Schock nicht enden darf', *Die Zeit*, 2 February 1979

by the last. Spontaneously varied as Furtwängler's performances sometimes were, they always seemed to grow from the
seed of their beginning: they sounded 'natural', if one grants
that the artist proceeds in a manner analogous to nature.

In an age such as ours which is fascinated by language and
linguistics it is easy to forget that organized thinking is
possible without the help of words. On his own purely
musical grounds, Furtwängler the conductor strikes me as a
'thinker' second to none; as a writer on music, on the other
hand, I rarely find him satisfying. 'I cannot,' as he says
himself, 'get involved with a work in order to demonstrate it
reasonably and with love – and at the same time talk about it.'
Yet there are a few instances where his words do reflect his
musical task.

> It is necessary that both the detail and the whole have gone
> through the performer's emotions. There are some who
> can feel a single phrase; only a few who can grasp the
> complete line of an extended melody; and nearly none
> who can do justice to the total context of that veritable
> whole which every masterpiece represents. There is,
> however, a way of dealing with compositions – overly
> practical and therefore universally adopted these days –
> which does not even attempt emotional involvement. It
> presents the bare facts without their meaning.

Another clue to the character of his conducting is
contained in a letter to his childhood mentor and lifelong
friend Ludwig Curtius. He writes: 'The work of art should be
a mirror not only of one's nerves, of the acuteness of one's
observation, the consequence, coldness and sincerity of one's
conclusions, or of the refinement of one's senses, but of the
whole man.'

Lean, bent slightly backwards, and with an elongated neck,
Furtwängler in front of an orchestra gave the impression of
overlooking vast spaces. His beat had very little in common
with that of present-day conductors. In stretches of pianissi-

mo it could be minute and extremely precise; elsewhere, outstretched arms undulated downwards in total physical relaxation, so that the orchestra had to guess where the beat should be. The sounds thus produced could be of an elemental intensity that I have not experienced since. The image of 'Jupiter tonans' was what came to me then: Furtwängler's thunder was always preceded by lightning-shaped movements, which made the orchestra play considerably after the beat (if there was a beat), and induced double-basses and cellos to prepare the ground for the sonorities by discreetly anticipating their entry. Arthur Nikisch, according to Furtwängler, was the only conductor who presented a thoroughly unforced appearance; Furtwängler regarded himself, in this respect, as Nikisch's pupil, and believed that any contraction of muscle on the part of the conductor would show up in the sound of the orchestra as if reproduced on a photographic plate.

Furtwängler's technique, though seemingly unfocused and impractical, was in fact well considered. Not only did it help to anticipate the quality of sonorities and the delay of an important beat: it also foreshadowed changes of atmosphere or the gradual modification of tempo. And this leads us to Furtwängler's particular strength: he was the great connector, the grand master of transition. What makes Furtwängler's transitions so memorable? They are moulded with the greatest care, yet one cannot isolate them. They are not patchwork, inserted to link two ideas of a different nature. They grow out of something and lead into something. They are areas of transformation. If we observe them minutely, we notice that, at first almost imperceptibly, they start to affect the tempo, usually a great deal earlier than is the case with other conductors, until their impact finally makes itself felt. Even where I disagree with the amplitude of Furtwängler's tempo modifications – as in the first movement of Beethoven's Fourth Symphony – I do not know what to admire more: the urgency of his feeling or the acuteness of his control.

Tempo modifications are merciless indicators of musical

weakness. With Furtwängler, as often with Casals, Cortot or Callas, they give evidence of supreme rhythmical strength. It would, however, be misleading to look at rhythm, or any other musical element, by itself. If rhythm is to be more than an abstract scheme or a crude obsession it must be influenced by articulation, character and colour. It must be affected by the performer's reactions to harmonic events and – a particular rarity these days – by that feeling for cantabile which permeates music in the widest possible sense.

Furtwängler made one aware of the interdependence of these and other musical factors. What is called 'structure' emerged as a sum of all the parts. Consequently Furtwängler's performances were often less idiosyncratic than those of his fellow conductors, and more varied. Listen to his recording of Beethoven's *Leonore* Overture No. 3 with the Vienna Philharmonic Orchestra, with its astonishing variety of colour and atmosphere, tempo and dynamics, character and meaning. Yet the music is never burdened by 'expression' from outside. Energies within the piece are released, the essence of the entire opera comes to life without the need for words. Ecstasy and strategy are perfectly matched, combining to produce the big line.

Furtwängler's big line is not a kind of long-sightedness, presenting the larger contours while the details of characterization are lost. It is one of Furtwängler's distinguishing features that, at least within the repertory he excelled in, each musical character is conveyed with a superior clarity of vision, and with the mastery of the superior professional. Even where the music seems to be left alone, where apparently 'nothing happens' during several bars of the softest playing, as in the cello tune of Schubert's Unfinished Symphony, conviction alone would not deliver such stillness. It had to be conducted and rehearsed.

It had, incidentally, to be recorded as well. There is a widespread belief that Furtwängler's genius was only present in live performances – a belief kindled by the maestro himself, who disliked recording sessions. The glorious Unfinished Symphony with the Vienna Philharmonic, a

performance as perfect as any I know, is only one of a
number of studio recordings that refutes this opinion. On
nearly all counts it seems to me more satisfying than the live
recordings I have heard. Equally outstanding are Schubert's
Great C major Symphony (Berlin) and Beethoven's *Leonore*
No. 3 (Vienna) which, judged as a whole, stand up to any
recorded live performance. And the studio recording of
*Tristan* seemed to have pleased even Furtwängler himself
who, for once, admitted that a record can have musical
merits. I wish Furtwängler could have known how much his
performances still mean to many of us today.

At the beginning of these notes I wrote of my debt to
Furtwängler for providing me with criteria by which to judge
a performance. Looking back over my remarks, I find I must
add some afterthoughts.

I have mentioned the variety of musical factors and their
interdependence. Let me add an example. Furtwängler's
pianissimo, extremely remote, yet without a meaningless
moment, was more than a degree of dynamic quietness; it
was a matter of colour, and Furtwängler's colour – even at its
most sensuous or nervously refined – was always a matter of
emotion. Thus *pianissimo* and *misterioso* were often identical.

I have hinted at the decisive importance of the very
opening of a piece, its dominating impact over what is to
follow – the way in which it reveals a particular musical vista,
causing one to enter a stage set for an inevitable dramatic
action. I have yet to declare my admiration for some of
Furtwängler's codas. In the concluding sections of the first
movement of Mozart's G minor Symphony or of Beethoven's
Ninth Symphony, he managed to make us feel that the life of
a piece had been lived through, and that the coda expressed
the tragic summation.

I have also referred to his ability to characterize, and to
change the chemistry of character and atmosphere during
transitions. One of my early piano teachers told me, with a
smile, that performers can either play beautiful themes or

beautiful transitions, but rarely both. Furtwängler made nonsense of that theory. He seems to me the exact opposite of Charlie Chaplin in one of his early films. Chaplin the pawnbroker carefully takes an alarm clock apart under the eyes of its owner; finally, when every single component lies spread out on the counter, he sweeps the lot into the owner's hat.

*(1979)*

# A Case for Live Recordings

My subject is a stepchild – live recording. Standing between the two officially canonized sources of musical experience, concert performance and studio recording, the recorded concert has had less than its due.

There has been a good deal of discussion about the differences and similarities between concerts and studio recordings. I should like to offer my own catalogue of distinctions (bearing in mind that a concert hall may turn into a studio if recording sessions take place in it).

In a concert one plays just once, in the studio several times if necessary. In a concert you must convince the audience at once; in the studio it is the accumulated result that counts.

In a concert the performance is only experienced once; in the studio it can be reproduced. In a concert the performer must get to the end of the piece without a chance to make corrections. In the studio he can make corrections, learn while he records and get rid of nerves.

The player before the public must do four things at the same time: he must imagine the performance, play it, project it and listen to it. In the studio he has the opportunity to hear it again after playing, and to react accordingly.

In a concert it is the broad sweep that counts. The studio demands control over a mosaic; while it offers the performer the possibility of gradually loosening up, there is also the danger of diminishing freshness. And there is the painful business of choosing between takes.

When playing before the public, details must be projected to the furthest ends of the auditorium, just as the whispers of an actor must be heard throughout the theatre. In front of the microphone one tries, on the contrary, to get away from exaggerations and aims for an interpretation that will bear frequent hearing.

In the concert hall the concentration of the audience brings about a mutual influence between the performer and his listeners. In the studio nobody has to be conquered – but there is nobody to disturb you. The player sits as though in a tomb.

A fit of coughing or the chirping of the alarm on a watch may break the spell of the most delicate moment of the concert. The studio offers silence.

Weaknesses in a concert performance tend to result from spontaneity, from a break in concentration or from nervous pressure. In the studio they may have their roots in excessive critical awareness.

The ability to convince the public in the concert hall is quite independent of absolute perfection. The studio is ruled by the aesthetics of compulsive cleanliness.

All these are observations from the player's point of view. Concert-goers and listeners to records may like to add that a concert involves physical presence, while the 'pure music' of the record avoids it (a bonus for those who suffer from agoraphobia or feel uncomfortable in crowds); moreover, the sound reaches the listener unmanipulated and as directly as the acoustics of the concert hall permit. The sound of the recording, on the other hand, is decided by the technical staff, the musical effect depending on such factors as editing, balance, reverberation and the qualities of the reproducing equipment. Lastly, not only must the player perform an entire work in a concert, but the audience must sit still and listen until it is finished. (People rarely leave a concert during a performance. Such respect for the concentration of both musicians and audience is one of the tacit agreements of a cultured public.) But when you listen to a record you can turn the music off, savour it in instalments or try bits here and there; you can move, talk, eat and groan – in a word, you feel at home.

## 'Accuracy and Soul'

Despite the funeral orations Glenn Gould delivered on concert halls, they continue to be the setting for the most vivid music-making. I do not wish to be dogmatic and will admit that there are concerts without a breath of life, and records of electrifying vigour. All the same, it follows from the way they come about that concerts are more likely to be characterized by spontaneity, tension and risk, studio recordings rather by reflection and superior method. To quote Robert Musil's *The Man without Qualities*, with its 'Generalsekretariat für Genauigkeit und Seele' (Administration of Accuracy and Soul), I may say that in the studio accuracy is more readily manageable than 'soul'.

Studio recordings have enormously increased the acuteness of detailed listening, including that of the musician listening to himself. In conjunction with the influence of modern *Urtext* editions and the demands of contemporary music, the gramophone record has profoundly upset listening habits. Its effect on the player, however, may not only be purifying but also sterilizing; it may be petrifying as well as concentrating and distilling. The interpreter who aims at accuracy risks less panache, lesser tempi, less self-effacement. The gramophone record today sets standards of perfection, mechanical not musical, which the concert hall seldom confirms. It induces some artists to play in a concert as though for a record, in the fear that the audience is listening as though to a record.

But a concert has a different message and a different way of delivering it. Now that we listeners to records and studio troglodytes have learned so much from studio recordings, it seems time to turn back and learn from concerts once again.

## Players and Public

For the sake of objectivity, let us consider the recordings of the 1930s, such as those of Cortot, Fischer or Schnabel. One may not have been aware then of certain imprecisions, in the way modern wrong-note fiends are. Where the leading of voices, the grading of dynamics, the control of character and atmosphere, timbre and rhythm are handled with the mastery of Cortot at his best, it appears to me that momentary lapses in concentration are not only irrelevant but almost add to the excitement of the impact.

In the 1930s people seem to have played in the studio almost as in a concert. But was this really so? Even then, players must have been worried about providing lasting evidence on a record, unless they could summon up the unbelievable nonchalance of a Richard Strauss. Apart from that, the limited duration of the 78 rpm disc was basically at variance with the nature of playing longer pieces as a whole. But then, as Emil Gilels told me about his own early recordings, a side may have had to be repeated thirty times if the producer so commanded, and the players had no opportunity to hear the results themselves, since a wax matrix was destroyed by one playing.

Above all, there was no audience. Why, if I may believe my own experience as a listener, does an impressive concert tend to leave stronger traces than a record? Because the listener, no less than the player, has had a physical experience, not only hearing the performance but breathing in it, contributing to it by his presence and sharing his enthusiasm with many others. The listener encounters the composer together with the performer and the rest of the audience in one place and at one time.

In the studio the player is alone with his own self-criticism and with the Argus ears of the producer. Even if he possesses the important gift of playing there with all the tension of the concert platform, and however vividly he might imagine the presence of the public, it is still imaginary. There is no direct exchange. He will, of course, try to remain as close as possible to his concert performances, using takes of a complete piece as a basis. But whoever subscribes to the belief that tape editing is a deception and that only complete takes should be used, deceives himself; he would renounce the advantages of

the studio and still fall short of the enchantment of the
concert, for it is not just the tension of the single uninterrupted performance that counts. (No one listening to my
records could tell which movements remained unedited and
which were put together from a number of takes.)

Here the live recording serves as a bridge. What is it able to
convey? For me, there is above all the attractive feature that
the uniqueness of a concert has been thwarted. The concert
took place on a certain day: the public was present, as we can
hear in the background, and we can imagine being present
ourselves – a fancy much less ridiculous than wishing to
imagine ourselves in the bare studio.

What you hear and enjoy is an indiscretion, something that
was only intended for those present and cannot be exactly
reproduced. It is not the technical level of reproduction I am
referring to: the fact that live recordings cannot always
achieve the quality of the best studio products hardly worries
me. It is the participation of the public, the aura of physical
presence, the contribution of which cannot be altogether
assessed on a live record; and yet, in some happy instances,
these leave their mark in the heightened intensity of a
performance, in the increase in the player's vision, courage
and absorption.

### 'Trouvaille' or Production

Why have live records been so rare until now, except for
those of famous artists of the past enjoyed by connoisseurs
and collectors? First, because a concert becomes more
difficult when it is recorded. The sight of microphones on
the podium does not fill the artist with glee. Incidentally, one
must make a clear distinction between radio recordings and
live productions for commercial gramophone records. The
former are more easily bearable since they will only be
broadcast once or twice, while the latter are bound to terrify
the player, being aimed at an international body of critical
contemporaries, and future generations. Live productions

are therefore only worthwhile in special cases, one of which I shall mention later. On the whole, live records should come about by chance; they should use radio or private recordings that give the artist pleasure. (Of course it is outrageous that, in some countries, they are still sold without the artist's agreement.)

Here we come to the second difficulty about live records: the prejudice against their alleged technical, and even musical, inferiority. Losses in digital quality and realistic balance, accidental noises, inaccuracies in the playing or fatigue in the instruments are mentioned as deficiencies that cannot be tolerated. True enough, there is no call to make a commercial record of a performance that has caught the interpreter off colour, the public during a flu epidemic, or a fleet of fire-engines passing by. Apart from that, the latest developments in recording technique will sometimes make an expert in electroacoustics happier than a musician. There are chance recordings that bring a piece of music to life and studio performances that destroy it. Those who consider spotless perfection and undisturbed technical neatness the prerequisite of a moving musical experience no longer know how to listen to music.

## Speaking for Myself

In pleading for live recordings here, I do not by any means wish to turn my back on the studio. I have spent innumerable interesting and some happy hours in it, owe it much essential experience, and shall continue to acknowledge my records, though with certain reservations. But in future I should like to place more frequent live recordings next to them. My first live record was devoted to the longest masterpiece of the older piano literature, Beethoven's Diabelli Variations. Since then I have been waiting for a suitable performance of the 'Hammerklavier' Sonata Op. 106, and recently found one in a London concert given in April 1983. Why am I drawn, of all things, to the biggest and most dangerous works? Because

they best provide evidence of a mastery that is not available
to some 'studio artists' and because it is works of that scope
which stand to gain most in boldness, absorption and vision.
The objection that no player can function uniformly well for
an hour or so, however justified in itself, misses the point of a
concert performance. Compared with the evened-out results
of the studio, it may show greater dedication and that
unexpected success that differs from a premeditated result
as a poem differs from a timetable.

## Beethoven in Chicago

Although I would not normally wish to make a planned live
recording, an exception came about in Chicago in June 1983.
On this occasion the effort of performing the cycle of the
Beethoven piano concertos was added to the risks of a live
recording.

Performances of cycles make the stature of a composer
more clearly recognizable. They are especially appropriate to
great composers like Beethoven, who constantly have something new to convey. The unmistakable character of each
movement, when played in close succession with the rest of
the cycle, shows its profile even more distinctly to performers
and listeners alike.

The Chicago Symphony Orchestra, James Levine and I
are old acquaintances. My contact with that splendid orchestra goes back to 1970 and has continued with welcome
regularity. The Ravinia Festival of 1977 gave us the opportunity to play all the Beethoven concertos under James
Levine. On the first evening the temperature was around
100°F and the humidity 95 per cent, which disturbed the
orchestra not a whit: concentration and control of the
playing remained virtually unaffected. The cycle was repeated two years later. Finally, in June 1983, two series of
Beethoven's concertos were recorded digitally in Chicago's
Orchestra Hall.

The undertaking had a double goal: we intended to

examine and to realize a concept of these works in several stages. The rehearsals were used to go, among other things, into the difference between *sforzando* and *forte piano*. Levine and I found ourselves in friendly agreement about what Beethoven's scores communicate, while the musicians of the orchestra never tired of re-examining pieces they had long ago mastered.

At the same time we hoped to document that tension and directness which manifests itself more readily before the public, a kind of spontaneity within pre-set boundaries which would rather discover than reproduce.

The confidence of all concerned in one another was the safety factor that made the risk of this live recording for once a calculable one, but it would have been extremely unwise, not to say foolhardy, if only for technical reasons, to have relied on the tightrope-walk of a single series of performances. The availability of two cycles gave us the possibility to combine some benefits of concert and studio: the freshness of the moment with the advantages of having a choice. I am not giving away any secrets if I say that live productions nearly always work in this way, seeking a synthesis or a compromise between both worlds.

All the same, despite every precaution, the audience could still have spoilt the lot. Over the years I can remember concerts with screaming babies (Japan), a barking dog (New York), a mewing cat (Istanbul), somebody falling down in a faint, a maniac clapping in the most impossible places, and a power cut plunging us all into darkness. (In Chicago itself I once had to stop during a recital, a few bars into the hushed beginning of Liszt's 'Sposalizio', and tell the audience: 'I can hear you, but you can't hear me.') None of these things occurred; on this occasion the exceptional stillness and concentration of the Chicago public filled me with gratitude. It was almost possible to forget how dangerously one lives when one records live.

*(1983)*

# On Recitals and Programmes

'Le concert, c'est moi.' When Liszt wrote to the Princess Belgiojoso that, in this pronouncement, he was affecting the style of Louis XIV, he had just launched a new type of public concert: the solo recital.[1] To be precise, the announcement in London used the plural 'Recitals on the Pianoforte', starting on 9 June 1840 – recitations of pieces of music, testimonies, one would guess, to both Liszt's declamatory playing and the romantic closeness of music and poetry. Hitherto, soloists had contributed ·to a programme that employed a variety of participants, including an orchestra. Joint recitals, rather rare these days, were still fairly frequent at the beginning of our century, when Busoni shared a concert platform with Ysaÿe or Melba.

Between each 'recitation' Liszt went to converse with people in his audience, a habit we have fortunately shed. (Another discontinued habit of old days, and a rather endearing one, was to modulate, arpeggiando, from one piece to the next; Wilhelm Backhaus still improvised discreetly in this manner.) While Liszt's newly created recitals may have lasted a couple of hours, some of Anton Rubinstein's mammoth programmes of the 1890s cannot possibly have taken less than three. Today we have settled on concerts of roughly eighty minutes' playing time, forty in each half. Of course, there may be the odd exception of a longer one, or a different balancing-out of the two halves, should an oversized work such as Beethoven's Diabelli Variations demand it.

How ought these eighty minutes to be filled? Of two standard programme schemes that come to mind, the old-fashioned one treated a programme like a menu: starter (or soup) and main course, followed by various salads and

---

[1] See Alan Walker: *Franz Liszt*, The Virtuoso Years (Faber, 1983), p. 356

puddings, and topped by omelette flambée. Artur Schnabel, in *Music and the Line of Most Resistance* (1942), wrote extensively about, and against, such musical meals. According to him, 'the first condition of a good menu is that all dishes should be prepared by the same chef or several chefs of equal merit; that all should be prepared with first-class raw materials, and that the gourmet should concentrate with the same seriousness on all of them!' The usual concert menu is far removed from these requirements. In my younger and more wicked days I invented, for an encyclopaedia, a list of compositions which included a work entitled 'Suite gastronomique'; during its last movement an omelette is supposed to be set alight on the performer's head. The bald virtuoso to whom it is dedicated has so far declined to give it a try.

The other standard programme scheme proceeds in a roughly historical order. Yet the reverse, or an apt historical mixture, is equally justified. I would accept no hard and fast rule in programme-making except one: that works in the same key should not follow one another. A varied succession of keys is required to stimulate the listener's attention. If the whole recital does not have a true key scheme, its sequence of pieces should at least be checked for suitability. I maintain, as Artur Schnabel did, that it is a mistake to connect in performance Mozart's C minor Fantasy K.475 with the C minor Sonata K.457. The fact that they were published in one volume proves nothing. Each of these works is an autonomous masterpiece; together, they cancel each other out.

A whole evening in one basic key is even more tedious. I once heard Beethoven's Sonata Op. 106 played after Schubert's D.960, both in B flat. It proved to be a miscalculation on every possible level. Even the succession of major and minor on the same tonic tends to be, in larger works, precarious. A combination as tempting as that of Beethoven's Diabelli Variations and his last sonata, Op. 111, should therefore be ruled out. But there is yet another reason: for both works, the only position within a programme that seems to me permissible is at the end. The Diabelli Variations present a complete universe, while Op. 111 leads irreversibly into silence. Encores, for that matter, are out of the question. I remember once seeing an advertisement for a recital that started with Op. 111 and continued with the Liszt Sonata. I cannot recall how the programme went on after the interval, and prefer not to recall the pianist.

The idea that recitals have to end brilliantly or mightily belongs to the past. If I ask myself how they should *begin*, my first advice would be to avoid pieces which may break the player's neck. To sit down and throw oneself into Schumann's Toccata may prove too much for even the most dextrous and cold-blooded of virtuosos. On the other hand, it would never have occurred to me to start a Beethoven cycle with Op. 28, as Schnabel apparently did. For this most relaxed of sonata beginnings I prefer to have settled down and thoroughly acquainted myself with the instrument. If I caution the player against immediately daring the devil I do not want to imply that I can tolerate the notion of the 'warming-up piece'. This notion suggests to me that the player has not seen fit to try out the piano or that the initial piece need not be taken quite seriously. Right away, the player ought to be fully involved and challenge the audience to share his or her concentration. Instead of playing down to an audience, the player should make the audience 'listen up'.

Good programmes are based on sufficient contrast. But they usually also reveal connections. Obvious connections are demonstrated when specimens of certain forms like the sonata, or of freer concepts like the fantasy, are assembled. In such programmes the diversity of possible solutions within a concept should become apparent. My own début recital ambitiously offered a choice of works from Bach to the present day, all containing fugues. Busoni, in 1909, toyed with the idea of two entire dance programmes, the outlines of which are given in a letter to Egon Petri.[1] As for a full

---

[1] See Antony Beaumont: *Ferruccio Busoni*, Selected Letters (Faber, 1987), pp. 96–7

recital of variations, here prudence is required. I have tried
out, and discarded, a programme of Beethoven's Opp. 34, 35
and 120 sets. The only successful variation programme I
could possibly think of is that of Mozart's Duport Variations,
Brahms's D minor variations from his String Sextet Op. 18
(in his own transcription for Clara Schumann), Liszt's
'Weinen, Klagen, Sorgen, Zagen' and, once again, Beethoven's Diabelli Variations – works in which the diversity of
the short span is absorbed in a comprehensive psychological
whole. Each of these sets is markedly different in its basic
character – graceful, heroic, suffering, humorous – as well as
in the technical treatment of its common formal idea.

Connections and contrasts of another sort were laid out in
a programme that tried to make a case for late Liszt. It
started with a selection of eight of his late pieces, interrupted
in the middle by Schoenberg's Six Little Pieces Op. 19 or,
alternatively, Bartók's *Naenies*. Half an evening of late Liszt
should, I imagined, prove not only possible but highly
rewarding. The juxtaposition with short twentieth-century
works would underline Liszt's modernity. After this group of
pieces, united in their opposition to classicism and functional
harmony, the second part of the recital was given over to
examples of neoclassicism or neo-baroque: Busoni's Toccata
and Brahms's Handel Variations. Busoni, having absorbed
influences of Liszt and Brahms, could be seen to have united
both worlds in the central Fantasia of his Toccata.

Depending on the performer's ability to switch from one
style to the next, a programme of extreme contrasts can be
hugely satisfying. On paper, the idea of putting three of
Liszt's Hungarian Rhapsodies between Fantasies by Bach
and the Diabelli Variations may seem perverse. In reality, the
profane complements the sublime. Not only do Liszt's pieces
hold their own surprisingly well; they also reveal, in their
quasi-improvised introductions, Liszt's familiarity with
Bach's improvisatory fantasies, and link Liszt's virtuosity with
that of Beethoven. After all, the Diabelli Variations display,
besides other things, a considerable amount of bravura.

*

It is amazing to what degree works (and composers) can be shown, by the context in which they appear, in a new light. If, in a programme of well-matched Haydn and Beethoven sonatas, Haydn's are played first and last, they are given a new status and might be listened to with different ears. When Beethoven's 'Appassionata' is presented – after works such as Haydn's G minor Sonata, Brahms's Ballades Op. 10, Weber's Sonata in A flat and Mendelssohn's *Variations sérieuses* – as the evening's conclusion, it almost sounds like a different piece, and certainly feels different under my fingers. This prog- ramme has a double effect: it upgrades not only a number of undervalued or lesser-known masterpieces but also the 'Appassionata' itself. Not that I have ever been one of those who have become wary of this great work's 'heroic' attitude, resentful of its popularity, or doubtful about its place among Beethoven's special achievements. But hearing it in close connection with Weber, Mendelssohn and Brahms, compos- ers who beside, or after, Beethoven had to find a voice of their own, may produce the sensation of watching all the pieces of a puzzle come together, and grasping what completeness is about. (Note: Weber's strangely neglected Sonata, the one basically graceful and radiant work in this generally dark programme, is placed in the middle.)

Among the programmes that I particularly enjoy playing are those that feature one composer only. When Clara Schumann heard Anton Rubinstein perform four Beethoven sonatas in one evening she deemed it inartistic. 'Doesn't *one* Beethoven sonata need one's entire soul? How, then, could one play four sonatas in a row with one's entire soul?'[1] On top of this, Rubinstein added a fifth as an encore. Unimagin- able what Mendelssohn or Robert would have said. Bülow's feat of playing Beethoven's last five sonatas en suite would have given Clara a heart attack. Admittedly, in taking on such an exhausting programme Bülow overstated his case. But, in his time, certain late works by Beethoven were still the property of a few – and every generation seems to have its

---

[1] Clara Schumann's Diaries, 18 February 1893

endurance tests. (At present, Messiaen's *Vingt regards* and Stockhausen's *Klavierstücke* might qualify.)

If the right composers and works are chosen, one-composer programmes should be far from monotonous. To me, there is a parallel with the major exhibition of a painter. Does he gain in stature when his pictures fill several rooms, or will this reduce the pleasure that we derived from seeing a few of his works interspersed between those of other artists? Here is my personal choice of keyboard composers whom I would volunteer to listen to on their own: Bach, Scarlatti, Haydn, Mozart, Beethoven, Schubert, Schumann, Chopin, Liszt and Schoenberg. Others would probably add Brahms, Debussy, Bartók and Messiaen; or Alkan, Ravel, Skriabin and Rachmaninov. I should advise against Carl Czerny, though – and I know what I am talking about; in the 1950s I had to sit through an all-Czerny recital which was delivered with missionary zeal by a friend of mine.

The range of what a great composer can express seems mysteriously incompatible with his limitations as a visible, and tangible, human being. I cannot imagine anything more thrilling than to explore that range. In works suited to fill a whole series of concerts, such wealth and breadth become gloriously evident – always provided that the performances rise to the occasion. At the same time, the individual character of each work is etched more clearly. Concerts in a cycle differ from single ones. In a cycle, the majority of the audience remains the same. There is a feeling of sharing, a cumulative effect, the experience of a spiritual journey jointly undertaken with the performer. With the end of the cycle, a goal has been reached.

While Schubert cycles are a relatively recent venture, and the first Mozart concerto cycle I know of was launched by Ernst von Dohnányi as late as 1941, all of Beethoven's sonatas had already been performed in the 1860s by Sir Charles Hallé, in 1873 by Liszt's pupil Marie Jaëll, and in the 1890s by Eugen d'Albert and Edouard Risler. Busoni's six Liszt recitals in Berlin in 1911 accomplished something that none of Liszt's own students had ever dared attempt. The first great pianist to survey the 'history of piano music' in seven recitals was Anton Rubinstein (1885–6). In the Beethoven programme of his series he surpassed himself, and even Bülow, by playing, in one go, Opp. 27 No. 2, 31 No. 2, 53, 57, 101, 109 and 111. Since the last war, Beethoven's sonatas have sometimes been done chronologically, a practice I find rather pedantic. Those who are interested in the evolution of Beethoven's style and range can pursue it with the help of records. In the concert hall, well-balanced contrast and a variety of style in each recital seem to me preferable. I would opt for a careful placement of the minor-key sonatas (a minority of nine), and for the distribution of the five late sonatas on different evenings.

Recital programmes may have to accommodate various necessities. What did I play when I visited a certain city the last time? What would I like to add to my repertory? Which works have been agreed on for future recording? Which twentieth-century works do I include? Is the recital part of a programmatic series, needing to be adjusted accordingly? Do I want to comply? Of such pressures and queries, a good programme should reveal nothing. Even if it subscribes to a guiding idea, a programme is a balancing act. The balancing is done mainly by instinct, helped by experience. More often than not, programmes explain, or justify, themselves only in retrospect. A basic disposition – whether to play it safe or to administer a dose of disquieting surprise to the public – will leave its imprint on the whole enterprise.

  In terms of repertory, two extreme positions are embodied by the player of hits and the player of oddities. The hit player, persuading himself that the best is also the best loved, caters for the biggest public attendance. The player of unfamiliar music, on the contrary, resents popularity as debasing or shies away from competition in the established field. Programmes of rarely performed works can be highly sophisticated and illuminating, or wonderfully dotty, as that of a violin solo arrangement (if I may, for a moment, switch my attention from pianists to string players) of Wagner's *Siegfried* dedicated to Cosima Wagner and performed at Wahnfried. The three final sections of this event, arguably one of the most indispensable one-man shows and one-composer programmes ever to hit the eardrum, were named: 'Siegfried on Top of Brünnhilde's Rock', 'Siegfried Awakens Brünnhilde' and, presumably in double stops, 'Siegfried and Brünnhilde'.

A close contender might be the piano recital given in Vienna in 1926 by a certain Wilhelm Bund. It started with a lecture in which Bund criticized the Viennese critics – all mentioned by name in the printed programme – and ended with a composition by Bund described as follows: 'Longing to die in voluptuousness – rearing and sinking back, shimmy-foxtrot as song of destiny, orgiastic dance (disrupted), exclamations of desire, desperate struggle, apoplexy.' I wonder whether Mr Bund survived the concert.

While such programmes are collectors' items, there are those that betray a collector's obsessive mind. We have the collector of fast notes, chords and octaves, of which as many as possible are supposed to be delivered per second and square inch; and the player of miniatures (*Lozelachs*, to use a Viennese pre-war term) who, abhorring larger structures, deals exclusively with musical bric-à-brac. Of these, Paul de Conne, a pupil of Anton Rubinstein and specialist in arranging tricky passages for fragile hands, piled up in one recital twenty-three pieces by seventeen composers, if I may trust my informant.

I would not want to bully anybody into anything. But I feel it ought to be a matter of personal pride for younger performers to play a fair share of the new repertory, and for older ones whose resilience may betray signs of erosion at least to listen to new works, and live in their aura. Among all the programmes I could name, those promoting important new music get my highest marks. Of course, as we live in an imperfect world, the attention and credit such concerts earn is often scanty. Few all-round performers will be able to muster the heroic dedication and specialized skills that are required to cope with a recent work like Ligeti's admirable Etudes. Yet this is precisely one of the tasks that a gifted young player should try to work at. To someone like myself who, as a performer, is absorbed by playing the old but enjoys listening to what is new with passionate curiosity, there is some consolation: the old does not simply have to be well lit and expertly preserved, like Titians in a museum. It continuously needs to be brought to life, and relate to our own time. If handled rightly, the result should be far removed from musical consumerism and mental sloth. Ideally, the performer should champion the neglected and the new along with established masterworks, and by no means exclude famous pieces just because they are famous. In his programmes, Maurizio Pollini has admirably stayed this course.

The piano literature, even if we only consider its finest works, is too extensive to be mastered by one single player. An intelligent and far-sighted choice of repertory is therefore paramount. Which are the works that one can plead for with conviction, that one hopes to grow into, that one would want to spend a lifetime with? Which is the music players can discover, or audiences ought to notice? Recitalists are rhetoricians; they have something publicly to convey. In classical rhetorics the main propositions are to instruct, to move and to amuse. The performer should not dodge the obligation to be edifying. His sense of quality has to inform the audience. In his programming, he should not give in to commercial demands. The more uncompromisingly a performer follows his own convictions, the better for his self-esteem and, in the long run, the esteem in which he is held by others.

'Le concert, c'est moi'? The programme is the player's visiting-card. But make no mistake – an intelligent, ingenious programme does not guarantee convincing performances. It still needs to be projected, generating a spiritual link between composers and listeners but also turning into an intense physical experience, an event unique and unrepeatable, tied to the day and hour, the sound of the hall and instrument, the sudden burst of sweat in a spasm of anxiety, and the bravely stifled coughing fit. All being well, the executant's grasp of his programme and his audience will be surpassed by the grip of an unseen hand that keeps its hold over player and listeners alike for the duration of a few timeless moments.

*(1989)*

# Bach and the Piano

## (with Terry Snow)

| | |
|---|---|
| TERRY SNOW | You have avoided playing Bach's works in concerts for a number of years. Why have you changed your mind? |
| ALFRED BRENDEL | The expert use of old instruments is a fairly recent achievement. I spent the post-war years listening, sometimes with a great deal of admiration, to the development and application of this expertise; the question was how convincing such performances would prove in the long run. Another thing was that I had studied with Edwin Fischer, whose Bach playing conveyed, in its own way, such powerful authority that I felt unable to free myself from its grip. The moment had to come when I became secure enough to deal with Bach on my own terms. |
| SNOW | This implies that 'historical' performances did not win you over? |
| BRENDEL | They didn't entirely. I feel that many of Bach's works are less dependent on the instruments of his day than are the works of Monteverdi or Domenico Scarlatti, of Purcell, Rameau or Couperin. And I think that a coexistence of 'historical' and 'modern' Bach performances is possible, and necessary. |
| SNOW | What are the advantages of playing Bach's keyboard works on the piano? |
| BRENDEL | First of all, the sound of pianos suits modern halls. That of old instruments does not. A critic |

who thinks that Bach performances should be confined to old instruments should also insist that one travel to a baroque marble hall to listen to them; or stay at home to hear them played on a record. Now, to my mind, Bach should remain part of the living concert repertory. Thanks to critical opinion his music has nearly vanished from piano recitals, and pianists are about to lose the skill of 'polyphonic playing', once held in high esteem, a loss that makes itself felt not only in Bach, and not only in dense contrapuntal structures.

Bach's keyboard music is full of latent possibilities. It is sometimes difficult to decide for which of his keyboard instruments a piece was written. The A minor Fantasy and Fugue, for instance, has many features of an organ work. There are, on the other hand, among his keyboard compositions typical ensemble pieces, orchestral works, concertos or arias which found their way on to the keyboard at the expense of more varied instrumental or vocal timbre, declamation and dynamics. They seem like a two-dimensional reduction of something three-dimensional. How did these works get there? Because one keyboard player can master a whole work alone without having to compromise with partners. The modern piano, thanks to its greater sensitivity to colour and dynamics, can sometimes restore this third dimension.

SNOW      Should the absence of interpretation markings on the autographs be remedied today by adhering to the conventions of baroque playing – with regard to the use of rubato, for example, or the choice of tempi and dynamics?

BRENDEL   On the piano, certain modifications of rhythm

and tempo are obsolete. There is a link between rubato and dynamics. Where the instrument does not permit phrasing and declamation to be moulded in dynamic terms, more rubato playing will be necessary to make the music breathe, particularly in cantabile music. There are, however, cases where the importance of a strict pulse will overrule all other considerations, as in the *perpetuum mobile* motion of the final movement of the Italian Concerto.

SNOW     Are there any characteristics of the harpsichord sound which you would consider reproducing, as, for example, the contrast of 'big' and 'small' registers?

BRENDEL     I do not hesitate to underline dynamic contrast with octave doublings where it seems musically necessary. Generally, however, I am more interested in suggesting those qualities of the music which stay dormant on Bach's instrument. And there is a special group of pieces of a prophetic kind, such as the remarkable A minor Fantasy, or 'Prelude' (Bach-Gesellschaft XXXVI/138), which seems to have been written for an instrument of the future in any case. As a harpsichord piece this Fantasy seems to me unsuccessful; as a piano piece it turns out to be quite marvellous, communicating surprises from bar to bar, never giving away to the listener where it will go.

SNOW     To look out for surprises in the music and fully employ the development in keyboard interpretation up to the present day – doesn't this inevitably lead to 'romanticizing' Bach's music?

BRENDEL     Not necessarily. Does any music convey the spirit of improvisation more immediately than Bach's Fantasies? Is not the execution of the arpeggiando chords in the Chromatic Fantasy left to the imaginative gifts of the player? I remember the days when the backlash against the excesses of 'romantic' performance resulted in unemotional and drily mechanical abstraction. Nowadays we hear Couperin on the harpsichord played in a way that amazingly resembles the 'romanticism' of Paderewski's records: no chord without an arpeggio and the left hand constantly anticipating the right.

SNOW     As for the use of modern dynamics ...

BRENDEL     Forkel's edition of the Chromatic Fantasy and Fugue, published towards the beginning of the nineteenth century and allegedly based on a tradition of performance handed down by Wilhelm Friedemann Bach, already contains many tempo changes and dynamic markings, including that huge, hideous crescendo over the last lines of the Fantasy which has been reproduced in so many subsequent editions. I think that some 'historical' performances, and the development of twentieth-century music, have led us to a new structural understanding of Bach's works, contrary to interpretations which indulged in values of colour and atmosphere for their own sake.

SNOW     Can you give an example?

BRENDEL     Since Busoni, the arpeggiando chords of the Chromatic Fantasy have often been played in a new, subdued and mysterious manner which to me is structurally unjustified.

SNOW     How important are transcriptions (such as those by Busoni) in translating Bach to modern instruments? Do transcriptions help to convey or impede the 'real voice' of Bach?

BRENDEL       I don't know about the 'real voice', but some of
              Busoni's versions of Bach's organ chorale pre-
              ludes do convey Bach gloriously, provided that
              one restores a few details according to the
              original text. Others at least give the pianist an
              opportunity to conjure up the sound and
              volume of an organ, plus the reverberation of a
              church. And, though it seems that the piano is a
              nearer relation of the harpsichord than of the
              organ, it lends itself much more readily to
              imitating the organ.

SNOW          Should the greater sonority and resonance of
              modern instruments place some constraints on
              ornamentation for modern players?

BRENDEL       It should, sometimes. And there is also the
              question whether the unadorned line may strike
              us as more impressive. Not that we should
              ignore those ornaments which are authentic.
              But we may use our own judgment and
              discretion about whether to add unwritten
              ones.

SNOW          Instead of slavishly reproducing practices of
              the past, should the Bach pianist examine
              former conventions of performance as to their
              validity to present-day ears and musical minds?

BRENDEL       Certainly, and he should ask himself whether
              they are tied to the musical structure, and
              contribute to the basic character of a piece. No
              'rules' of performance should be automatically
              applied. Does a string player really have to swell
              out each tenuto note as much as the bow
              permits? Should he turn every two-note group
              into a vehemently accented sigh? Even if it had
              been a passing habit to emphasize certain
              rhetorical elements, we may find them of minor
              significance today. Rhetorical elements have

always been an important part of a good performance. If they are over-projected, and given undue prominence, they sound – to my ears – hysterical. Music, instead of speaking, shrieks and moans.

SNOW Does it make any sense to say, as Nikolaus Harnoncourt did, that music before the French Revolution was primarily rhetorical and declamatory, after the Revolution emotional and atmospheric? Do we really have to choose between declamation and the big line, or between logic and atmosphere?

BRENDEL I do not see these elements as alternatives. They are interdependent and balanced out in a masterpiece. The performer, on old or modern instruments, should try to reveal this balance.

*(1976)*

In the years following this interview, amazing things have happened. The virtuosity in dealing with period instruments is now staggering. There are 'period orchestras' – reaching in their repertory even beyond the Age of Enlightenment – whose precision and refinement matches that of splendid conventional ones. They can even play in tune. Convincing balances have been found. The brass does not invariably attack you full blast, and the timpanist is not encouraged to perforate his instrument – at least by some conductors. The best of these conductors, mellowed by experience, do not need to overstate their case in order to prove their point. Principles, textbook rules and fixed ideas are held in check by musicians for whom music is the sum of all its parts. Performances have become less dogmatic and more personal.

At the same time, the pianists have rediscovered Bach. Mainly thanks to András Schiff, his piano music has re-established itself in modern concert halls, to the delight of

listeners and executants alike. A coexistence of 'historical'
and 'modern' performances is now taken for granted. And
what is more, there is a true cross-fertilization: 'authentic'
conductors have learnt to compromise with 'modern' players,
while these players in turn have taken up suggestions by their
'authentic' colleagues. There are advantages on both sides,
and it is wonderful to see how enemies are about to become
friends.

*(1989)*

# On Schnabel and Interpretation
## (with Konrad Wolff)

KONRAD
WOLFF
In the preface which you wrote for the new editions – in German and in English – of my book about Schnabel's interpretative ideas on piano music,[1] you say at the end that what you feel about these ideas is 'admiration' on the one hand, 'opposition' on the other. I want to ask you about the substance of your opposition, for two principal reasons (apart from sheer curiosity).

First, you have become the first pianist since Schnabel – two generations apart – who again enjoys full authority in the field of interpretation of Mozart, Beethoven and Schubert. (Your other repertoire was hardly shared by Schnabel.) Secondly, in the opinion of many, and also in mine, your approach has much in common with Schnabel's, both in details of phrasing, tempo and dynamics, and in your basic attitude, and this against a different approach by nearly everybody else. Yet, when you played the G major Sonata of Schubert the other night, you told me afterwards that you did everything contrary to Schnabel's rules, or words to that effect. He would not have been aware of a disagreement except in details.

There is one basic point where I see a very different approach between you and Schnabel, but I am sure we shall get to it.

---

[1] *The Teaching of Artur Schnabel*, A Guide to Interpretation (Faber, 1972)

## 1  *Metre, Rhythm and Tempo*

ALFRED
BRENDEL

What I remarked about the G major Sonata was mainly referring to its beginning. I remember one of the examples in your book which suggests that the G major chords, as they are something like the spine of the beginning, should be played with a certain amount of weight whenever they come. I don't agree, because I think that if one plays the last chord with weight instead of 'taking it away', the roundness of the phrase is gone. This brings me to some metric articulations by Schnabel – his idea that in a phrase there are one heavy bar, two light bars and then one heavy bar at the end, or at least a light bar in the third bar and a heavy bar at the end. If one were to apply this to this beginning, I think it would be contrary to what I see in it.

I see in this beginning a whole phrase, and by phrase I mean something like a curve, a bridge which starts down here and then goes up into the air and leads down again. So what interests me about phrases is often much less the counting of the bar-lines and the functions of bars, but the whole shape. In another example from your book which is supposed to illuminate the heavy-light-light-heavy scheme, the C minor episode in the finale of the G major Sonata, Schubert's own accents tell the player to do the exact opposite:

Only the minuet theme, for once, adheres to Schubert's pattern. I think what Schnabel does with his metric articulation is to overestimate bar-lines. Very often for me the art of phrasing consists of forgetting about bars, ignoring bars and seeing large unities. If I think, for example, of Schubert's B flat Sonata, then I think that the whole point of playing the beginning is *not* to disclose where a light or where a heavy accent may be, not to disclose where there is an upbeat (is it just the first upbeat or does it lead to the next bar-line?); to play as if this theme would have to continue something which had been going on for some time already. The music really has begun already and one sits down and continues something. One does not emphasize the upbeat – one leaves the mystery of how the theme is organized undisclosed! By leaving it undisclosed it becomes more mysterious, in my opinion.

WOLFF    That is beautifully said, but I don't think you have the slightest disagreement with Schnabel – especially with this beginning. I believe I mention in my book that he thought of it as a 6/4 bar that starts one beat before the first note.[1] Schnabel is the one who said, 'If I were rich enough I would have all my music printed without bar-lines.'[2] I don't think it is the

[1] p. 71
[2] p. 99

bar-*line* that he emphasizes. Rather it is two
things, really. One is that he wanted to know
how far he was to play before there was a
breath (the length of the breath – including
harmonic rhythm); the other is that he said that
a phrase begins and then goes *from* there, or
else it ends and goes *to* there. He also said that
in every phrase either the beginning or the end
is the more important.

BRENDEL     Well, there are two things I should like to say.
I'm sure that Schnabel did not have such a
simple mind that he had simple rules. Everything I know about him suggests that he often
contradicted himself and had new ideas about
the same things – he even wanted, to a certain
degree, to amaze his pupils and confuse them,
thus showing them in how many ways the same
music may be understood and how the person
may change who performs it. But I find several
references in the book, and I hear, sometimes,
certain things – not so much in his own playing,
but in the playing of some of his pupils – which
tell me that he must have taught a bit of this
bar-line business.

WOLFF       All our music is filled with the numerals V or
III, where he dictated to us – or wrote himself –
that the metrical period in question was five or
three bars long.

BRENDEL     And yet within his periods he loves to emphasize bars: 'light bars' or 'heavy bars'. Now, for
instance, there is an example at the beginning
of Beethoven's Op. 2 No. 3 where he wants the
first four bars to be heavy, light, light, heavy,
which to me is absurd.

Why should the dominant be light and the tonic at the beginning and the end be heavy? If anything, for me, it is the opposite. If we look at the piano writing of this opening we find one tenth in the left hand, in the third bar. This tenth for me indicates the high point of the whole phrase. Then it relaxes, because with all the energy of this beginning it still has a certain graceful quality about it. I think that what Schnabel attempts to do here sounds a little bit forced.

The other thing is that when I listen to his playing, and the playing of some of his pupils, I find an organization of the playing which refers to what you said about thinking about how long the breath should be and where a new breath should start. I'm not sure that I agree with this kind of musical thinking at all. I feel that inasmuch as the pianist should sing inside himself, and on his instrument, he should not accept the physical limitations of a singer. I would go further and say that the singer himself should not accept his own limitations. When the singer has to breathe, he should do it in a way that is as unobtrusive as possible. There's a lot of music – for example the vocal music of Beethoven – which does not take into account the breathing of the singer at all. The singer has to be, like a very good instrumentalist, able to bridge all those gaps where breath is necessary. There is such a thing as 'accented breathing'. It should only occur where the drama of the music requires it, not as a matter of course.

Also, for me, Schnabel's playing sometimes likens music too much to language, with full stops, commas and all. Music is not as simply organized as that. Even when it has a very eloquent quality – a speaking quality, a telling quality – it does not have sentences or commas or the organization of words into rhythms in a way that would make it easily comparable to language. Obviously Schnabel himself knew better, according to your book. 'Where something new begins, something old is continuing all the same. This is the first clue to the idea of phrasing. The last note of one phrase is frequently the first note of the next ...' I totally agree. Very often there are several things going on at the same time. You may have a *melodic* ending and *melodic* beginning, but there may also be a *harmonic* ending and a *harmonic* beginning which is so important that a breath, a musical comma, would take away the necessary continuity. For example, at the end of Beethoven's C minor Concerto, in the coda, you have the presto theme.

WOLFF        Somewhat Rossini-like?

BRENDEL      Yes, and there is something like a downbeat at the end, a *forte* downbeat of the orchestra which I have sometimes found corrected in the orchestral parts into *mezzo forte*, because somebody saw in it only the end of a phrase. In actuality the new phrase starts there as well. There is a switch of phrasing. This is the *forte* platform for all the downbeats which happen later. I have very rarely heard it played energetically enough to project the meaning of the whole end. So I feel that *Punkt und Komma* in musical interpretation is an undue simplification of musical matters. I shall always remember a performance by a very well-known trio of the second movement of Beethoven's 'Archduke' Trio. There was a horrible little stop after each four bars.

WOLFF    I love this phrase, because Beethoven leads to a *forte* in the fourth bar but not in the eighth.

BRENDEL    Yes, indeed. Even after eight bars such a stop would be horrible. Such slight separations of phrases are sometimes taught. They disfigure the rhythmic context. For me, it is much more interesting to connect phrases than to separate them, as a principle. That is something I have probably acquired from my teacher, Edwin Fischer, who did not speak about this in such terms but would demonstrate it all the time.

WOLFF    I have been sort of forced into the role of the Boswell or Eckermann of Schnabel (a role in which I don't feel adequate, especially not now after forty-five years), and I don't know what he would have said about it. As for me, I agree with all you have just said. Only I think that in the music before Beethoven, and especially in Mozart's music, there is still a great deal of *rhetoric* tradition stemming from the time when instrumental music was really a surrogate for vocal music. The speaking, the recitative-like quality, like the sighing motives of Mozart's music and some other music of the time, is much greater, and I see one of the principal innovations of Beethoven as being that he created an abstract rhythm that was not to be filled with words.

BRENDEL    I want to repeat that a lot of my musical thinking is vocal. And I find, especially in Mozart's piano concertos, many operatic traits which make me treat the piano part in as vocal and declamatory a manner as I can. Yet the operatic singing of Mozart has also changed quite a bit in the last thirty years. I think this is probably the greatest change in musical performance which has happened during our lifetime. If I listen to Beecham's *Zauberflöte* nowadays (recorded in the 1930s) it's a very strange experience. The style of the singers could hardly be tolerated today.

WOLFF          I agree – there has been a gradual change.

BRENDEL      And yet I would expect that even a singer could create the big line, could connect whatever he had to sing. 'Connection' is not even the right word. What I mean is that one thing leads into another. This is an area where I sometimes disagree with Schnabel's playing – the area of rhythm and tempo. What I am sometimes missing is the rhythmic continuity. He is very much concerned with clarifying harmonic progressions, and with giving the impression of declamation – even in passage-work.

WOLFF          Also with melodic rise.

BRENDEL      And with, of course, the melodic organization, but often unconcerned with purely rhythmical matters – the importance of an even, rhythmical flow.

WOLFF          This is exactly what I had hoped you would get to because this is the point, mentioned earlier, where I do see a difference in approach. To illustrate, I want to tell you that Schnabel once admitted in a lesson that, as a game, he sometimes would have, especially in slow movements, a metronome going when he practised and he would try to play as rubato as possible against the metronome so that he would come together on every strong beat – but be entirely unfettered between beats. I don't think you would do that.

BRENDEL   I would possibly do it in slow movements which have a speaking quality and where one of the main features of the music is not a regular rhythmic pattern which has to be maintained. I do not think that where there is a regular accompaniment it always has to be as strict as in a Stravinsky piece. But let me get back to one of the examples in your book. You talk about the harmonic articulation in the Brahms D minor Concerto, in the coda (Più animato) of the last movement.[1] Of course, I also know Schnabel's record, and I think that the rhythmic articulation he suggests and plays there is harmful because the overriding importance is the regularity and energy of each little beat. It is one of the most disturbing aspects of some of his performances that the rhythmic priorities are sometimes not accepted, or recognized. For instance, towards the end of the C minor Concerto by Mozart, wherever there are broken chords, Schnabel lumps them together harmonically in portions and separates them from each other. Similarly, wherever there are broken octaves, he will not play them evenly but plays them like grace notes before the main note. These things happen so often that one gets the impression of mannerisms, of bad habit. It is something, I have the feeling, which he failed to control.

WOLFF   Sometimes he probably did, but in the finale of the Beethoven C major Concerto it was his way

[1] pp. 90 ff.

of showing how Beethoven foreshortens the phrases. Of course it was not out of control. It had a musical purpose. It may have been the wrong means ...

BRENDEL   Let me put it differently. The musical purpose is too thickly underlined. Musical ideas cannot be presented as fixed ideas. Schnabel's treatment of rhythm too often gives me the feeling ... well, that he thought a continuous rhythmic pulse was boring. There is a matter of principle in his playing where principle should not come in.

WOLFF   He had a great fear, which came out in his teaching, in his criticism of his students, of being what one usually calls 'notey' – that one would hear too many single notes. He always quoted a negative review that he had had many years earlier, where a critic wrote, 'His semi-quavers sounded like peas counted by a prisoner.' Apparently that was what he wanted to avoid under all circumstances. Do you have some of that same fear – of playing one note after the other in fast music?

BRENDEL   Well, first of all I wouldn't listen too attentively to critics. I try to make out what the music requires. There may be a situation where evenness of rhythm is essential. I think this is more often the case than Schnabel's playing would disclose. But does evenness of rhythm exclude expressive playing? Wasn't it Schnabel who, when asked 'Do you play with feeling or in time?' responded: 'Why shouldn't I feel in time?' But let me go on to another matter. The central area of my disagreement with Schnabel is not the treatment of rhythm, it is the treatment of tempo.

WOLFF        Yes. It is probably a generation difference too.

BRENDEL      I ask myself whether this is the case. If I
             compare performances of other great players
             of Schnabel's generation, like Cortot and Fis-
             cher, then I find that fast movements and fast
             pieces are often played faster than some people
             would dare to play them today, whereas the
             treatment of slow tempi varies. For instance,
             Cortot never played extremely slowly in his
             whole life. Not that I missed it, but he got away
             without playing a real Largo. Fischer tended to
             play slow movements fluently, particularly
             Andantes, and told his pupils that there is a
             marked difference between Andante and a
             really slow movement. On the other hand he
             could expand the tempo of a Largo, as the one
             in Beethoven's First Concerto, to wonderful
             effect. With Schnabel I get the impression (and
             he says so in the book) that he wants extremes
             of tempo. He suggests it to be a virtue to play a
             slow movement slower than anybody would
             expect. He also suggests that it is an interesting
             way to amaze the listener to start a fast
             movement faster than the listener thinks one
             can manage, and I have the feeling that he is
             really doing that in some of his own perform-
             ances. Here I do disagree. I think that playing
             music as slow or as fast as possible makes music
             into something bordering on sport.
                 Dealing with tempo, as with dynamics, as
             with colours, as with every means of musical
             expression, there should be as much variety as
             possible at the command of the player. There is
             an enormous variety in all music and the player
             has to look for it. Preconceived ideas will limit
             his or her possibilities. To concentrate on
             extremes of tempo means to neglect the wide
             area of tempi in between.

WOLFF       May I say that you simplify his approach to
            tempo a little bit. For instance, in certain
            symphonic first movements, he tried to have
            the tempo slow enough to have the music
            develop with a certain majestic quiet. The
            examples that come to my mind are not from
            piano music but chamber music. In two B flat
            trios, the 'Archduke' and the Schubert B flat, he
            usually criticized everyone for being too fast in
            the first movements. There again he was not
            quite alone in his generation.

BRENDEL     And yet if I think of the recordings I have
            heard, of most of the Beethoven sonatas, the
            general impression remains of extreme tempi.
            Of course, I ask myself whether he always
            played like that, whether that was his intention,
            or whether a certain amount of nerves made
            him play too fast and, in slow movements,
            extremely slowly.

WOLFF       You must remember that records in those days
            were only about four minutes long, and there-
            fore the tempo of slow movements was occa-
            sionally slightly modified for recordings. For
            instance, I don't recall the slow movement of
            the Beethoven Fourth Concerto played as fast
            by him as on his record. It had to fit on two
            sides.

BRENDEL     This is a great pity, because it is an Andante con
            moto and I think it should be played flowing!
               I remember being told that Schoenberg was
            listening to a performance of Schnabel playing
            the Beethoven C minor Concerto on the radio.
            There was the first chord of the slow move-
            ment, then the second one never came, and
            Schoenberg said, 'I can't count any longer!'

## 2 Sound

| | |
|---|---|
| BRENDEL | I never heard Schnabel in the concert hall. I only have second-hand experience from the records. |
| WOLFF | I heard him often in his house and in the concert hall. In my opinion, the pirated records are the best reproduction of his real sound. |
| BRENDEL | I must say that from the records I do admire his sound very much. It is one of the reasons why Schnabel is a constant source of inspiration to me. And yet when I read through your chapter about regulating sound I have to disagree with certain ideas. For example, does the piano tone remain the same throughout the entire range of the instrument? I ask this because on the pianos of Beethoven's and Mozart's time this was certainly not the case. The interesting thing is that the bass sound and the treble sound and the sound of the middle range sometimes differed nearly as much as the voices of a string quartet would differ. There was enough variety to exclude the statement that the basic characteristic of the piano was the evenness of the sound, an evenness which inspired composers to take this into account as a basic quality of the instrument. Of a first-class modern piano I would expect that in dynamics and quality the sound should remain similar throughout the registers. It is then up to the pianist to produce the necessary variety of balance and timbre. And I think that not only the listener should imagine sounds of other instruments coming from the piano; the pianist has to imagine them and produce them in the first place. |
| WOLFF | Well, if I didn't say that in the book, it is a bad |

omission, because certainly Schnabel wanted that.

BRENDEL    Unlike the harpsichord or the organ, the piano sound can be moulded in many ways. 'In the great majority of compositions for the piano I think the composer wanted his music to sound like piano music and nothing else.' This is a quotation from the book, and as far as I am concerned the contrary is probably true. I would think, if I looked at the latent possibilities in most piano works, that piano pieces are rather reductions. They are usually reductions of musical ideas which belong to the orchestra, to chamber music, to the voice – whatever you name. A reduction so that one player, without having to compromise with others, can master them – at a price. I think the price should be as low as possible. The present-day piano lowers the price more than older instruments could – with a few exceptions.

It is interesting that in your book there is little talk of Liszt. Schnabel in his last decades did not play him in public, I think.

WOLFF      I never heard him play Liszt, but when he was young he played the Mephisto Waltz and the Sonata – and I think the Second Concerto.

BRENDEL    He seems to have enjoyed teaching Liszt, as you have written. Liszt, of course, makes the pianist aware of all the purely pianistic possibilities of the piano. If I have a principle it is in agreement with this one – that the piano, in itself, is not enough. That it is an instrument not with a strong character of its own, like the human voice or a string instrument, but rather like a character actor – it wants to play roles. It can turn into nearly everything you can think of. So much for principles.

| | |
|---|---|
| WOLFF | You said today's piano lends itself more to most piano music – with certain exceptions. What are the exceptions? |
| BRENDEL | There would be pieces like certain Haydn sonatas which need a particular bite and clarity. They sound more idiomatic on the early Hammerklavier, which has still retained part of the harpsichord sound. There is music like Scarlatti which is very close to the hard edges of the guitar (after all, he lived in Spain for some time). It needs very clear contours, Mediterranean clarity. Returning to the word 'timbre' which I used a little earlier, I have written down a quotation from your book which says: 'Obviously, with the exception of the soft pedal, the piano has no means of altering its timbre.'[1] That again is something I cannot easily agree with. |
| WOLFF | This you can blame on me. Schnabel is not responsible for that statement. Of course this is meant as a *physicist's*, not as a *musician's* statement. |
| BRENDEL | I would think that the touch, the dynamics, the right pedal can also alter the timbre to a great extent, even to the extent of clearly suggesting certain instruments or certain combinations of players. |
| WOLFF | I once read in a Hindemith book that it makes no difference on the piano whether it is touched with the tip of an umbrella or with the finger of Artur Rubinstein. It is an argument that is very hard to refute in a convincing way, although we all don't believe it. It is true in a way and untrue in another – and that is what I |

---

[1] p. 157

was talking about. When you strike the key with the tip of an umbrella the only difference in timbre will be if you put your left foot down or not.

BRENDEL        Let's examine this. I think what is important is the *connection* between sounds. If you make single sounds it can possibly be argued that one sound is like the other, no matter what strikes the key. (Though, on second thoughts, even this is not correct. You can strike the same note softer or louder, faster or slower, gently or violently, with or without the pedals; this already gives it a certain amount of character.) But when it comes to the connection of sounds the matter looks entirely different. It needs fingers, it needs feelings, it needs a musical temperament and brain to produce what makes music worth listening to. Then all the elements like harmonics, the pedalling, the articulation come in to alter the sound, to alter the meaning even of single notes because they live within a certain context. Of course, if you like the piano played like an automaton – there was a period in the 1920s when composers tried to achieve exactly this, i.e. Hindemith in the Suite (Op. 26) – then the pianist can produce this too. But there's little piano music to which this treatment does justice. And the pianola can do better.

WOLFF          How do you react to Schnabel's rules for the ratio of loudness within chords?[1]

BRENDEL        I think that the ratio of loudness of chords depends very much on the character of the music. For example, at the beginning of the

---

[1] pp. 159 ff.

'Waldstein' Sonata you have four-voiced chords. If you play them in the manner recommended in the book (the soprano and bass leading and the middle voices slightly in the background) you will get a great deal of clarity but a totally wrong atmosphere. The atmosphere of this beginning is *pianissimo misterioso* ...

WOLFF In the book there are several categories, if I may contradict you, and you have to find the right category. The category where they are all in the same register, as is the case in this beginning. The category of the soprano and the bass being stronger than the inner voices would not obtain but, instead, the category is where they all belong 'to one family'.

BRENDEL Yes, but even with chords in the same position it is imperative to see which colour is required, which atmosphere, which distance (I mean that space-like quality which music can convey). In the case of the 'Waldstein', it is not daylight but dawn, I would say, not bright energy but mystery – even within the strict rhythmic pulse – and for me that tips the balance in favour of the inner voices. I play the inner voices slightly stronger than the outer voices. That makes the chord sound softer. This is an important matter. If the outer voices are played louder than the inner voices it does not sound pianissimo, no matter how soft you try to play them. The inner voices, in certain positions, give the *dolce* character, the warmth. Within a chord of four voices the interval of the third is the lyrical voice, the fifth is the horn – the mysterious voice – so if you have the normal position of a chord from C to C it would mean that the player who is interested in this poetical approach would favour, rather often, the middle voices and not, for instance, the bass line. I personally feel, after listening to pianists like Cortot, Fischer and Kempff (who in his best playing is a supreme master of sound and of balance), that to bring out the bass line is usually unnecessary. It is the basis of the harmony, of course, and it should be controlled perfectly, but it only needs to be pointed out where it denotes energy or where the bass has a special melodic or motivic or atmospheric importance. Otherwise, in music with functional harmony every musical listener will hear the bass more or less automatically, even if it is played very softly.

WOLFF        Yes, that is the difference between you and Schnabel which I have also sometimes noticed when you play.

BRENDEL      Yes? Sometimes my bass line is perhaps too soft?

WOLFF        It sometimes seems that way to me.

BRENDEL      Yes?

WOLFF        I can't recall a recent occurrence where it seemed so to me, but several years ago there were moments.

BRENDEL      There were, yes. I realized that myself and hope I have corrected it. I still think that to favour melody and bass as the two most important components of musical writing is, in practice, not always very successful.

WOLFF        My father was an old-fashioned music lover, especially an opera lover. I remember him saying that he didn't like to listen to Schnabel because he heard the left hand too much. Of course, that was the generation of the 1870s.

BRENDEL     Well, it depends on many things. If the piano
piece presents the sound of a soloist with an
accompaniment, then the melodic voice has to
come out very prominently – more prominently than nearly anybody dares to do it today. For
me, Cortot is an example of a player who could
bring the melody to the foreground with a
whole orchestra in the background without
losing the different timbres and voices. And
without ever forcing the sound. I should also
like to mention balance rules for the playing of
octaves, of which Schnabel says that they are
usually duplications of the main voice. From
the standpoint of part-writing this may be very
true, but as a principle of giving more value to
the main voice during the performance, I
would not always agree. Again, when I think of
the orchestra, when you duplicate something in
a score, the duplication may be in a stronger
timbre and may, by its strength and by its
intrusion into the purity of part-writing, give
special significance to the octave. I would not
accept the principle that in an octave there is
necessarily one leading voice and an accompanying one. There are octaves where both
notes have to be exactly equally loud, sounding,
so to speak, like one instrument. There are
octaves where the inner voice, even in melodic
passages, comes in like a duplication with a
horn. For instance, let's take the Schubert G
major Sonata, about which we talked earlier –
the beginning of the first movement. I do not
play the upper voice louder than the octave. I
favour the sixth in the right hand and make the
high voice accompany, gently, and that gives
warmth and body to the sound, whereas if I
were to bring out the soprano it would, to me,
sound too direct.

WOLFF        But Schnabel thought, I believe, as he usually
             did in such cases, of the third on top, like a
             soprano and alto singing in duet, and that's why
             he took the B in the left hand – the B below
             middle C.

BRENDEL      But then, what is the role of the thumb in this
             theme? There is a continuity of colour in the
             line of the thumb, and nearly all of it is a
             doubling of the soprano. It should sound
             particularly relaxed, and it lies so well in the
             hand. Why interrupt this continuity?

             To my ears, the sound of thirds and sixths
             should often be on the dark side. That means
             that the lower voice in Schubert and Brahms
             has to be at least as prominent and expressive as
             the main voice – particularly in minor keys. If I
             listen to the slow movement of Schubert's B flat
             Sonata, at least the thought that the inner voice
             is the most meaningful is valuable to me, even if
             it is not louder than the soprano. Maybe it
             comes just a split second after the soprano and
             thus draws imperceptibly a little attention to
             itself.

WOLFF        I hear and enjoy these things when you do
             them. The other day you did something ex-
             traordinary and beautiful. In the B flat Im-
             promptu (Schubert D.935, No. 3), just before
             the end, is a sforzato that I am always afraid of.
             You played it so that it was a sforzato but it had
             no violence, no harshness – you gave it the right
             dose.

BRENDEL      I changed the balance. That, for me, is often
             the solution and there is no secret about it.
             Other people have done it before. If I look at
             the accents of the A minor Sonata (D.784), in
             the second movement, they are not positive
             accents which stand out dynamically; they ask

for a change of colour in favour of inner voices, which gives the impression of pointing to a particular meaning or conveying something which is more private than anything before.

WOLFF    To end, let me ask you this: is there any one point or points, in general, where you think that Schnabel's doctrines, in the way I have tried to explain them, are still valid and important?

BRENDEL    Your question tells me that I must have given the impression of being entirely critical. I apologize! The subject of our conversation was to find out where Schnabel's approach, as you put it forward, differs from mine. I often feel close to Schnabel: when he speaks about general matters I usually share his opinion. When he goes into certain details of performance, such as rhythm and tempo, I sometimes have to disagree. I would say that the majority of things in the book are totally natural to me. I estimate that I would accept about two-thirds of your book with joy, and leave one-third open to discussion. And with all my queries, it remains the most stimulating and thought-provoking professional book that I have read in many years – to be precise, since Schnabel's own *Music and the Line of Most Resistance*.[1]

*(1979)*

Looking through this interview ten years later, I feel that I should add a few more instances of my dissent, if only for the sake of argument. Musicians who prefer to remain unaware of what they are doing may look at such scrutinizing as a

[1] Princeton University Press, 1942

useless contest in cleverness. This, I think, would not be quite fair. Konrad Wolff's, and Schnabel's, focus was on the discussion of musical matters, not on the promotion of personal glory and superiority. So is mine.

In the opening of Schubert's B flat Sonata, Schnabel 'wanted to avoid any point of gravity prior to the second downbeat' (p. 71). But is the second downbeat a point of gravity?

'Beethoven's rare pedalling instructions are without exception essential to the musical structure' (certainly not all of them) 'and do not leave any liberty to the performer.' Schnabel believed that, in these passages (Op. 31 No. 2, I, recitatives; C minor Concerto, Largo; 'Waldstein', finale; G major Concerto, I; Bagatelle Op. 126 No. 3), the 'bass note must be audible until the next bass note is played'. I cannot see why the C minor Largo should qualify. And how about Op. 126 No. 2, and Op. 106, II? 'If the pianist chooses the appropriate tone proportion and tone colour there will be no disturbing confusion in sound' (p. 84). Listening to Schnabel's record of the 'Waldstein', I have to voice my doubts. Under no circumstances should Beethoven's pedal markings be ignored. But these were the early days of pedal notation. In Beethoven's pedals the idea, whether structural, declamatory or atmospheric, should be conveyed, not the letter. There are ways of doing this without sacrificing transparency.

Talking about Mozart (pp. 102 ff.), Schnabel maintained that there should be no addition to the text. 'The pianist must play the exact number of notes the composer has written.' I would say that the pianist must give this impression (which is not quite the same!) unless there are patches that demand, or permit, elaboration.

On embellishment, 'the most important factor is the preservation of its decorative character'. There are embellishments which are decorative, and others which become part of the melodic line or have structural implications. 'Schnabel himself always played embellishing notes, and more *leggiero* than the principal ones.' I am afraid he did not.

In his recordings they often draw all the attention towards themselves. And his highly personal, very fast trills often sound uneven by emphasizing the lower note. (Liszt had a name for it: 'Kartoffeln abladen' – unloading potatoes.) Should trills not be varied, in speed, colour and dynamics, to fit into their musical surroundings? There are plenty of different trills, if one listens to Edwin Fischer or Kempff, and a good many of them have preserved the nature of an extended appoggiatura, meaning that the higher note must not be neglected.

Schnabel avoided 'playing measured trills and turns exactly coinciding with the figurations of the left hand'. An idiosyncratic statement, to me unacceptable as a rule. Schnabel claims that 'a left-hand staccato does not exist in Mozart'. In Mozart's notation it does, though only when motivic ideas of the right hand are played by the bass. Accompaniments are sometimes slurred, but mostly un-marked; then they should be adjusted to the context. When in piano concertos the orchestra plays the same theme with staccato accompaniment, the soloist will usually comply, as in K.414, III.

'The brilliant figurations in Mozart's concertos ... have to be played legato. This rule is practically without exception, since they are modelled on vocal coloratura and not on violinistic articulation' (p. 108). Why should they be modelled on vocal coloratura alone? And why should vocal coloratura not include articulation which a woodwind player or violin player would make? The nineteenth century considered legato playing to be standard practice (see Czerny's Piano-forte School Op. 500, and the old Mozart complete edition). Paul Badura-Skoda, on the contrary, is convinced that Mozart's passages have to be played non-legato unless they are slurred. I cannot accept either prescription. For me, the model instruments for Mozart's passages are the woodwinds. (In Beethoven's early E flat Concerto this kind of articulation is written out in detail.)

'Quick notes, following a dot, in so-called dotted rhythm should neither be played as part of a triplet, nor double-dotted.' They can, and often have to, be varied according to character, and rhythmic surroundings.

Schnabel, during a crescendo, 'would not admit any drop in loudness between beats, not even in the event of two-note phrasings' (p. 112). Why not? I see the completely even crescendo rather as the exception, the crescendo that incorporates smaller declamatory dynamics as the rule.

'Ritardandos should only be made where they are marked.' In another essay[1] I have reproduced a list of unmarked opportunities for ritardando, or ritenuto, given by Czerny in his Pianoforte School Op. 500.

If, in contrapuntal music, 'two equally important parts are to be brought out with equal clarity, they should not be played equally loudly'. Agreed. But 'in a two-part setting the lower of the two parts must always be softer than the upper' (p. 160). No, it must not. Either way is possible.

The performer should be 'shedding a surprising new light on the composer's deepest meaning' (p. 169). I am worried about the stress on 'surprising' and 'new'. Is it not difficult and absorbing enough to look for 'meaning', and to distil its essence? To surprise oneself, or let oneself be surprised, by musical discoveries is legitimate and satisfying as long as such discoveries illuminate the purpose of the piece. The intention to surprise one's audience, however, breeds eccentricity. Wanting to be different, the player easily exaggerates what is right or contradicts what is necessary.

I never met Schnabel, and do not belong to the legion of his enthralled pupils. Yet he remains one of the great musicians I relate to, both in admiration and in criticism. I should like to close these pages by quoting some of Schnabel's (and Konrad Wolff's) statements I am only too glad to share.

Schnabel 'always encouraged students to find out as much as possible about the structure, harmonies, motivic tech-

---

[1] *Musical Thoughts and Afterthoughts*, pp. 34–5

nique, etc., used in each score. But there is no basis for interpretation in most of this ... To *begin* the study of a new work by analysing its form, in school-term paper fashion, is more harmful than helpful ... True analysis is but a clarification and intensification of musical sensitivity, an additional push in the right direction as established by musical instinct' (pp. 18–19). Like Schnabel, I feel that few analytic insights have a direct bearing on performance, and that analysis should be the outcome of an intimate familiarity with the piece rather than an input of established concepts. At the same time, 'every music student should be obliged to write music, whether or not he is gifted for it or attracted by it. Such an obligation is, unfortunately, not even recommended nowadays, although it was a matter of course in former times' (Schnabel, *Music and the Line of Most Resistance*).

'He easily associated this or that section of a composition with pride or humility, outdoors or indoors, morning or evening, privacy or officialdom, cold or heat, remoteness or directness, agitation or sobriety, etc.' (p. 127). To be able to put into words matters of musical character, colour and atmosphere implies some kind of a literary effort. We need not only to understand what words mean and to feel what they suggest, but also to stretch the scope of our vocabulary. As Schnabel's (or Wolff's) examples show, the perception of contrasts is our starting-point. But let us not forget that they need not be mutually exclusive; there are, indeed, areas of overlapping, of musical twilight, as in several of Haydn's themes. And many characters are complex rather than clear-cut.

'It is a mistake to imagine that all notes should be played with equal intensity or even be clearly audible. In order to clarify the *music* it is often necessary to make certain *notes* obscure' (p. 157). Complete and permanent clarity of execution is a manner of playing which, instead of serving the music, is content with itself. It happens to be the beau ideal of most record producers.

'The performer's inner ear hears everything twice: each little bit is mentally anticipated as well as checked out by later control. If all goes well, these two perceptions are blended into one or, as Schnabel phrased it: "The conception materializes and the materialization redissolves into conception."' An event as mysterious as parallel lines meeting in the infinite. If all went well, Schnabel made them meet.

*(1989)*

# Index